Going Downhill

A Retiree's Guide to Ski-bumming

Linda Fawke

Acknowledgements

Many thanks go to family and friends who have allowed me to write about our joint experiences. Without them, there would be no book.

My main critic and reader is my husband and I can't thank him enough for his patience, valid (but gentle) criticism and continual support (even when I write late into the night). I'd also like to thank Jonathan Veale for his review of my book and his encouragement.

I belong to the Wokingham Writers' Group who support and critique my work and are, I hope, making me a better writer. My thanks to them.

Finally a big thank you to Fiona Routledge who created the book cover for me.

Also by Linda Fawke

A Taste of his own Medicine

A Prescription for Madness

For my grandchildren –
Maria, Lukas, Olly, Jamie, George, Idris and Ioan

Today's and tomorrow's skiers.

Note to Readers

This book is a snapshot, an account of our experiences over a period of around fifteen years. Please do not regard it as a traditional Guidebook – in spite of its title. Places change, restaurants close and new ones open, as do shops, hotels and services. Yes, the mountains are constant but the pistes on them may not be.

Just enjoy it as it was!

Why Not?

You can spend it in the garden. You can sit in front of the telly. You can sleep till midday. Retirement is a sad word. I didn't want to tire, with a 're' or otherwise. I was more for a re-firing and luckily we had the possibility of doing something adventurous. Work behind us, we would head off to the Alps for a surfeit of skiing, a second career as ski bums. Dreams are great while they are just that but the calendar, the mirror and the pensions people at work were pointing us to the end of our working careers. This dream could become real. 'Bit scary' as our little grandchildren would say!

I was apprehensive about giving up work. I loved it, loved the responsibility, the people, the chance to make a difference. So why was I even contemplating early retirement?

'Whatever will you do with yourself?'

'You're such a busy person – how will you slow down?'

'I can't imagine you not working!'

'I'll miss the click-click-click of your heels as you rush from place to place.'

These were the comments that bombarded me when I announced my intentions, so it wasn't surprising I struggled with mixed emotions as the 'R' day approached. I

1

knew I needed to be busy, that retirement wasn't synonymous with doing nothing, but how it would pan out was worrying.

Would I miss work?

Tony, my husband, had already retired, having changed his status without a backward glance. It's sickening how well-adjusted some folk are. I really didn't want, 'Wish you were here!' messages as he travelled the world while I ploughed through the e-mail mountain on a grim Monday morning. Okay, sometimes the job wasn't marvellous. His plan was to take me off to the mountains a couple of days after leaving work for the last time to stop me thinking too much about what was happening. So that's what we did.

'You'll be okay. You'll enjoy yourself. Don't worry. Retirement is good.'

We've skied in many places and been to the French Alps frequently, to Méribel Mottaret in the Trois Vallées, in particular. We have a small apartment there, so in many ways it's home to us. But we'd never been for more than a couple of weeks at a time and I was hesitant about being there for a whole season, a period of nearly three months. Tony had no doubts. He's one of those guys who are at the lift before it opens in the morning and bliss for him is finishing the day at the top of the mountain with a *vin chaud*, then skiing back down after the lifts have closed. It's partly ski fanaticism, partly the desire to make up for the first thirty-five years of his life before he learned to ski and partly determination to get his money's worth out of the expensive ski pass.

Tony knew me better than I knew myself. We set out in early January on our ski-bumming career. This is our experience.

Our First Season

Châteaux and Fine Dining

Four o'clock in the morning, two days after finishing work. We were getting up to go to the Alps. We didn't need to leave early but Tony can't bear to waste precious hours. He'd insisted retirement was one long holiday, but still booked a ridiculously early ferry.

'You realise that the person who makes us get up in the middle of the night has to do the driving?'

'No problem. I didn't expect anything else.'

I shivered as I left the house, clutching my pillow, and slept in the car. In fact, I'm not sure I really woke up until we arrived in Dover. There's a lot of France between Calais and the Alps and we wanted to discover some of it, instead of rushing through by the most direct, motorway route. Our plan was to break our journey at interesting places, spend a night or two here and there, and enjoy the leisure of not hurrying. Our arrival in the snow would be delayed but we would be relaxed and the journey would be part of the holiday. Places that were just familiar names, road signs, would become more than that.

The profile of the church at the town of Laon in Picardie was a familiar sight, high up above the motorway. We decided it would be our first visit. It turned out to be a delightful, mediaeval place. Tony forbade me from complaining about the four o'clock start and pointed out all the advantages it had given us. He was right.

It was chilly but we were going even chillier. We descended into tunnels under the town, wondering at the complex catacomb and sophisticated layout, most of which is open to the public. The tour guide asked, in French, if there was anyone who didn't understand French.

'Wonder if she realises what a silly question that is?' Tony whispered. 'If you don't understand, you can't answer!'

I did say we were English but should be able to manage. Would we? I worried whether my O-level French, topped up with a few conversation classes, would be adequate, not only for this tour but for future challenges. School didn't teach plumbing French or car-breakdown French or disputing-a-bill French. But these were problems for another day.

We were the only foreigners and our language abilities were at full stretch but the sights alone were impressive. Imagining the life of a wretched prisoner in the Middle Ages didn't need much French. An hour and a half later we returned to daylight and a little warmth; we were starting to discover the real France.

It was time to move on but I didn't know Tony's plans. He wanted to surprise me and I was happy to wait. Burgundy is directly in the path to the mountains so it was an obvious choice for our overnight stop. We arrived at the Château de Gilly in Vougeot, a previous abbey, stately and magnificent as an abbey should be. It sits in extensive formal gardens and the approach is impressive.

'All this has been here so long and we've just ignored it with our mad journeys through France.'

'Are we actually staying here?'

'Yes. Look what retirement's offering us!'

Tony was watching me, waiting to see my reaction. I

6

sensed he was worried I'd still have my mind on work.

'You're convincing me.'

We arrived to find we had been given a room upgrade although had no idea why. The room had a shabby, historic feel about it, inviting us into another, older world.

'Are we going for fresh air and frogs or stuffiness and silence?'

The closeness of our room to a pond full of frogs did mean we had to make a choice when we went to bed, but it all added to the atmosphere. Ornate furnishings, beamed ceilings and rich colours completed the ambiance. The restaurant was in the crypt with its arched roof and muffled atmosphere. We contemplated the extensive menu and wine list. I looked at the prices, worried it wasn't only our language abilities that were being stretched. You could spend significant money but you didn't have to. We chose a set meal which looked great to me although Tony was unhappy about snails for the first course. He's not a snail man. A word with the head waiter and it was substituted with something he preferred. We did, of course, toast each other with Burgundy in Burgundy.

The area is filled with vineyards, all offering tastings, confusing the traveller with an impossible choice. We asked for a recommendation and selected one of the nearest to visit the following morning at Marsannay. We arrived early and felt somewhat disreputable waiting at the entrance, like queueing for the pub to open. A nominal charge gave us a tour of the cellars and a few tastings. Our guide, Jules, then ignored what we'd paid for and let us try whatever we wanted. I think he appreciated our efforts to speak his language. I decided long ago that if I waited until I spoke perfect French, I'd never say a word. So I try at every opportunity. While we were sipping, another English couple arrived and asked to taste a rosé of a particular vintage.

'Would you like to try one of the whites as well? Or

another rosé?'

They refused to taste anything else, insisting this was the one they liked and would buy. No amount of encouragement could persuade them otherwise. The concept of there being only one wine worth drinking was so alien to Jules, he was almost speechless and struggled to keep his expression impassive. There was some shrugging of the shoulders and an eye-roll behind their backs. I'm sure we tried their share. Inevitably, we bought some wine, but why not?

We were not far from Beaune, the beautiful capital of the area. It has an air of affluence, the smart shops too expensive for me but it costs nothing to look. The buildings have red and gold rooftops and the Hôtel-Dieu, a previous infirmary built in the fifteenth century, is still in immaculate condition. The individual cots for patients, lined up along each side of the main room, with an altar at the end so that everyone could join in the services, were furnished with original materials. Mannequins of the nursing nuns stood beside the patients, each of which had their own set of eating implements, bowls and cups. No one knew at the time that this scrupulous attention to individual ownership was the best way of preventing the spread of infection. Those treated here were lucky but there were few of them.

There are many wine merchants in the town itself, with assorted visits to *caves* on offer. Tempted again, we called in one to find the receptionist too preoccupied with her phone call to talk to us. We decided out-of-town visits, like Marsannay, were better. You can be sure of a welcome, the attention is more personal and you feel you are supporting individual growers and wine-makers. When we left Burgundy, it was for the last part of the journey to the Alps; the snow was beginning to call.

Not all our trips through France have been as pleasurable and we talked about how we used to travel. We had a pattern when working of leaving our offices at four o'clock on a Friday evening, driving to Dover to catch the first available ferry, then continuing through the night, arriving at our apartment around lunchtime on Saturday. This enabled us to squeeze an extra half-day's skiing into our week as we headed straight for the slopes. Before we had our own apartment, we sometimes changed into ski clothes in the car park if the accommodation wasn't available. Our keenness knew no bounds and this maximised our holiday. Although we shared the driving, we still needed to stop for a few hours' sleep en route. It wasn't worth booking into a hotel as it was hardly a night, so we found a quiet *aire*, reclined the seats, locked the car and slept.

This worked well many times until we had an experience that totally altered how we travelled. While asleep in an aire near Lyon, we were awoken by the sound of breaking glass. I was covered in shards and we saw several black-clad men running off and jumping into a car which rapidly disappeared. My handbag had gone. It was black, by my feet, and the interior of the car was also black. Hardly visible to a casual observer. We were in an unlit part of the car park so we assumed these were experienced thieves searching the cars with a pen torch. My handbag contained both our passports, some English money, my credit cards, a cheque book, my electronic organiser, my mobile phone, my glasses and sunglasses as well as the usual random assortment of items every woman's handbag holds. A kind German lorry driver phoned the police for us who arrived quickly. They asked us to follow them to the nearest police station which we were about to do when we discovered one of the front tyres had been slashed. How lucky we'd been! It could have been one of us at the receiving end of the knife. I'd not even had time to be afraid, it all happened so quickly.

9

The police kindly replaced the tyre with our spare and we gave them all the information we could. They sent us on our way, a significant drive still to complete. The temperature was around minus five and we had no window in the passenger door. We tried rigging up a towel to keep out the cold but that helped little and was a lot less transparent than glass. So frequent warming-up stops at aires were inevitable. At the third one, a group of Dutch lads saw our problem, told us not to worry, pulled out a large roll of polythene sheeting from their car and made us a makeshift but effective window. We were bowled over by their kindness. We'd experienced mindless theft and selfless generosity within a few hours.

Ultimately, it was just an annoying inconvenience (it took me three years to gather all the addresses I'd lost). From then on, we travelled during the day, often arriving late in Mottaret, and sacrificed half-a-day's skiing. The aire where all this happened, Mionnay, still gives us shivers and we don't stop there.

Arriving late at the apartment brings problems, too. We arrived around midnight on one occasion to find we had no running water. This was the first visit of the winter and all had been well the previous summer. Judging by the number of cars in the car park, there were plenty of other occupied but dark apartments. At that hour, we could hardly knock.

'There must be a tap somewhere that's been turned off.'

'It's not under the sink. Try under the washbasin in the bathroom.'

'No joy. What about the loo?'

We looked everywhere without success. At this point, we both had raging thirsts.

In desperation, we searched the cupboards and found a part-bottle of flat tonic water. It was exquisite. The following day, having consulted the dictionary for words like 'stopcock', I was on the phone to the agency which acts as our *Syndic,* or Residents' Association. It looks after several buildings and their services. As a result, I discovered a cupboard in the entrance hall to the building. During some maintenance in the autumn, our water tap had been turned off and not turned on again. Another lesson learned.

As Tony pointed out, we now have no need either to sleep en route or arrive around midnight. We are retirees and can take our time!

At Home in France

Buying an apartment was our Millennium Project. Although retirement would be years later, our children persuaded us – easily – that we should not wait that long.

We knew it had to be in a large ski area where there would be plenty of variety to meet the needs of a whole season. Assorted ski holidays directed us to The Three Valleys – *Les Trois Vallées*. But where exactly? There was a vast choice.

Property in the Trois Vallées is expensive relative to the rest of the French Alps. So we knew buying wasn't going to be as cheap as in a smaller resort – and none of the good deals for renovation that were around in rural France. We weren't aiming for a project, anyway; we have enough of those at home in England. The intention was to buy a place we could use immediately as we were both still working, with limited and precious holiday allowance. All we knew was that we wanted to be in this part of the Alps.

Decision-making isn't one of our strengths and our last house move in England took some time. We're better if there is time pressure so we decided to put pressure on ourselves. There was a limit to how many times we could afford to travel just to look, anyway. The plan was to fly out twice in May 1999, on each of the Bank Holiday weekends, the first to look and the second to buy. And that's what we did.

The first surprise was booking accommodation for our short stay. We phoned a few tourist offices to discover the resorts were closed in May. It hadn't occurred to us that whole resorts close. We had to stay in a 'real' town, so we chose Brides les Bains as a good setting-off point. I phoned up a small *pensionat*, booked ourselves in for three nights and explained that we would be arriving late on Thursday evening, driving from Lyon airport. The owner told me the keys would be placed in the post-box behind the flowers, enabling us to get into the building and our room. It all sounded straightforward and we arrived around midnight.

The place was a blaze of colour with flower pots everywhere. The whole building and everything associated with it was 'behind the flowers'. We found a post-box but there appeared to be no way into it. I began to doubt my French – had I understood correctly? I was sure the owner had said *'derrière les fleurs'* but maybe it wasn't a post-box but something else. So we systematically began to look behind as many of the flowers as we could, under the pots themselves, under watering cans, bits of wood, chairs, sun umbrellas but without any sign of keys.

'We'll have to phone but I bet they've gone to bed. We're not going to get a friendly reception.'

'Well, what else can we do? It's too late to book ourselves into anywhere else. We'll freeze if we sleep in the car.' We were already suffering from numb fingers.

So I tried the phone. I really didn't want to, but I dialled the number, anyway. As there was no reply, we assumed the guest number didn't ring through to the private accommodation. Or they were sound sleepers. With little hope of success, I tried the post-box once more and to my extreme relief found I'd been trying to open it the wrong way. We found the keys.

It was a charming place. Old, basic and totally French but just what we needed. The room was small with a tiny, modern bathroom installed in the corner. The balcony onto the main street was the traditional wrought iron type, just big enough for two straight-backed chairs. We sat there with a glass of wine in the evening sunlight and watched the bustle of locals below us going about their lives. As the chambermaid was off on Saturdays, Madame asked us if we could make our own bed that day. Breakfast was the usual croissants, bread and jam, fresh and delicious, with hot, strong coffee, served in a large dining room furnished with heavy, dark furniture. Not a word of English was spoken. It was a wonderful start to our French adventure, the events of the previous evening just adding a delightful frisson.

We immediately set about a tour of the main resorts of the Trois Vallées. We wanted to be in the trees, so that eliminated Val Thorens. We found Les Menuires ugly, so that was out. Courchevel 1850 was too expensive and we didn't like the other two Courchevels at 1650 and 1550. These are more modest places than their higher neighbour, and although the newer buildings are more sensitively built, they do have their share of charmless, high-rise, flat-roofed buildings. So this left us with five resorts, Le Praz, La Tania, St Martin, Méribel and Méribel Mottaret.

'How are we going to decide?'

'Well, let's talk through what we do and don't like'.

'I like Le Praz and the apartment we viewed had a superb view of the ski jumps. It was beautifully fitted out, as well.'

'Mmm. But a bit too expensive. And Le Praz is at 1300m. We'd have to take the lift down at the end of the season. It wouldn't be skiable. No last vin chaud at the top of the mountain and skiing down after the lifts close!'

'The same applies to St Martin. Another proper village but low.'

'Higher than Le Praz. But we've not seen a property there we like.'

'I think La Tania's more promising. We get more for our money there.'

'Yeah, it's cheaper but it's low as well.'

In the end, reliable snow won and we sacrificed the desire to be in a 'real' village. This left Méribel and Mottaret in the middle valley, the *coeur* of the area. It was clear that being central was sensible. Access to Courchevel on one side and Val Thorens, Les Menuires and St Martin on the other would be easy and should the weather deteriorate with the risk of summits closing, there'd be a better chance of getting home.

Méribel felt too big and although we looked at some possible properties, none was near a lift. High on the list of requirements was nearness to both the lift system and a bread shop. We were planning for the days of old age when our mobility would be reduced. Mottaret, higher up than Méribel, a pretty place with a noticeable absence of concrete, was rising to the top of the list. One property in the Chatelet area, in the Alpages du Mottaret development, was promising. However, this was the 'looking' weekend; a decision wasn't necessary yet.

We returned at the end of May, having organised various viewings, including the Alpages place we liked. We stayed again in the little pensionat in Brides, key finding being simple this time. By Sunday morning, we were down to two properties in Mottaret, the one in Alpages and another nearby. We went through all the pros and cons and decided on the one in Alpages. It had the nicer layout, a better balcony and was in an attractive building. It was also more reasonably priced but a bit smaller. The larger one had a better view as it was higher up the mountain. Both overlooked Mont Vallon, a superb pointed mountain with two excellent pistes on it. Elated to have made the decision, we decided we had time to go for a walk. We set off past the Lac de Tueda and for the first of many times walked up the winding path past L'Aiguille du Fruit, a craggy scree-covered mountain, in the direction of the Refuge du Saut. We turned after about an hour as there was a flight to catch. We then made a mistake.

'Shall we just have one more look at both apartments again from the outside?'

'I thought we'd made our minds up.'

'We have, but it'll just confirm we're right.'

We felt satisfied driving past the Alpages building that it was a wise choice. Should we even bother to look at the other one? It was hardly out of our way, so we did. Mont Vallon looked beautiful bathed in evening sunlight – the view was better from the higher point. So we then spent the journey home debating whether we'd made the right decision. We decided Tony would phone the French estate agent at nine o'clock on Monday morning with an offer; which property the offer would be on was back in the melting pot. We had thinking to do.

As planned, just before nine on Monday morning, Tony called me at work.

'Have you decided?'

I asked him the same question. We both said 'Alpages'. And there have been no regrets. Some negotiations resulted in our becoming the owners of a furnished apartment. This was to be our base, our new 'place of work', for our ski-bumming careers.

The surprises had not finished, however. We tried to get a list of what the owners were leaving as we were buying the apartment furnished but there seemed to be a lack of understanding as to why we needed this. Once the place was ours, we understood their confusion. They had left everything, plates, cutlery, saucepans, pictures on the walls, bedding. There was little they removed from when we saw it. Our definition of 'furnished' was not as comprehensive as theirs. It meant we could use the place immediately and gradually replace what we didn't like. Tony didn't even notice the original curtains were hideous. On the practical side, we used an English lawyer with experience in French property sales. We were not expecting problems as the apartment was only three years old, but we decided to play safe. We also used English in all our dealings to ensure we didn't miss anything, especially if legal French was involved. The final signing for the property took place in Le Touquet on the north French coast where the owners lived. We met up with the notary and Monsieur the vendor for the final formalities. The notary and the vendor were obviously friends, chatting and sharing jokes. I made the mistake of smiling when something amusing was said.

'Vous parlez français, Madame?'

The notary had registered my reaction. In spite of my replying, *'Un peu,'* he refused to continue in English. As far as we know, we didn't miss anything critical. It just remained to collect the keys. They were, it seemed, with an estate agent in Méribel. We had a problem as we were intending to drive straight there, arriving late. Did the vendor not have any? Oh yes, he did. Bizarrely, he had not thought to bring them. So we drove to his house where we were left with their whippet (I learned the French for a whippet – *le whippet*), while he and Madame turned the place upside down to find the keys, eventually located in a vase.

***

As we approached Mottaret from Burgundy on our first visit as retirees, we were glad it was a Thursday. The traffic ran smoothly, no Saturday queue of tourists, no impatience, no swearing. Even after making many such journeys, there is always a thrill as the first mountains come into sight. Just south of Lyon, we could see the mountains around Chambéry, pink in the late afternoon sun, the snow glistening on the peaks. It isn't just skiing that makes the Alps wonderful.

'Just think, this is all because of Norway. If we'd never lived there, we mightn't be here now.'

'You're right. We may never have skied and would certainly not have been addicted!'

Initially...Norway

Our skiing careers began long before retirement and Norway has a lot to answer for. In the early eighties, Tony's work offered him the chance of going to Scandinavia. One evening he came home to our usual chaotic house where three young children had made their mark. After getting them to bed and a cursory tidy-up, he clearly wanted to talk.

'How do you fancy a few years in Norway?'

'Wow! Really? When? What's the deal?' My head was full of questions, excitement and apprehension.

'I'd go in a couple of months. You could follow with the children at the end of the summer term. We'd be in Oslo.'

'A lot to think about, but...' I paused for a few moments. 'Yes, why not? It's easier while the kids are young.'

They were five, seven and nine, portable, flexible and persuadable. I'd made my mind up quickly, almost on impulse, and I think Tony had already made up his. Any difficulties were for another day. So he said yes and we set about arranging the myriad things that have to be done when a family moves to another country. The children were excited without fully understanding what was happening. They latched on to certain key facts: it would be cold in winter with plenty of snow. They would learn to ski; we would all learn to ski.

'Mummy, how do you fasten skis on?'

'I don't know. I've never seen any skis close up.'

'Will we be able to ski where we live?'

'We'll be able to ski somewhere near, I expect.'

I really wasn't much use when it came to answering questions about a sport I'd never tried, had no idea if I'd like and hadn't a clue about the equipment needed. Usually, when children learn something new, their parents teach them. When I first took my kids swimming, I wasn't afraid of the water and was a reasonable swimmer. When they started riding bikes, I could help, even though my rear end and a bicycle saddle never really got on well. Now we were all going into unknown territory. This was a strange feeling.

Tony duly disappeared off to Norway ahead of us in early May. National Day in Norway is on 17th May and is a huge event for everyone. So his timing was good. A group of Norwegian colleagues invited him to go with them to celebrate in Finse, a small town high up on the Oslo to Bergen railway line. One of them had a *hytte*, a wooden cabin, out in the wilds near there, where they would stay. They said he needed cross-country skis as there was a plan to ski as well as celebrate. Neither of us had appreciated there was more than one kind of skiing. We had a depth of ignorance to overcome. Tony phoned me up to tell me all his news.

'I have to borrow some cross-country skis. Apparently, they are lighter and thinner than the alpine variety. You can go uphill as well as down on them.'

'So that isn't what we watched on TV?'

We had avidly watched a programme about skiing recently.

'No. That was downhill skiing.'

'I thought skiing was skiing. I suppose I'll learn!'

As everyone in Norway has several pairs of cross-country skis, the ones they use, their old pair and often their even older pair, Tony was easily able to borrow some. However, he decided he should buy some boots. Buying footwear is usually a major trial as he has broad, size six feet (yes, size six!) with a high instep. Shoe boxes fit him better than shoes. Never having tried cross-country skiing, he had no idea what he was looking for but, amazingly, he found some boots that fitted. They were rubber and were reasonably comfortable, looking rather like walking boots with a front extension that clipped into the ski binding. The heel was free. He was feeling pleased with himself that he had so quickly got into the Norwegian way of life. We later discovered no one wore boots made of rubber, but at that point, it didn't matter.

There is a saying in Norway which translates as 'born with skis on their feet' and the Norwegians are proud of their prowess on the narrow, cross-country planks. This is something they learn as infants and is what they consider to be real skiing. There is an element of scorn towards alpine skis, especially amongst older folk. However, the flip side of this is they can't understand anyone not being able to ski. It's a bit like my saying to a friend, 'Would you like to come for a hike? Oh, by the way, do you realise that you need to put one foot in front of the other in order to walk?'

So no one thought about any instruction for Tony. That he managed at all was amazing – and he recounted this story several days after he'd recovered (and has told it many times since).

Armed with my equipment – skis, poles and boots – and feeling pleased I'd managed to equip myself so well, I joined the group at Oslo railway station on the eve of the big day. The first let-down was the series of funny looks my suitcase attracted; everyone else was wearing a rucksack. Oh, well! Maybe the next item of equipment to buy? The train trip to Finse was wonderful – the best introduction possible to the wonderful Norwegian landscape. I chatted to

21

Peter, another English guy, someone with all of four months' skiing experience. *He sensibly suggested the two of us go out for half an hour after we arrived so that I wasn't a total ski virgin the following morning. Hardly what you'd consider comprehensive training but I was grateful for his help. As well as being narrower than alpine skis, cross-country skis are much less stable, wobbly even. Mine were, anyway. On the plus side, you can walk easily on them on the flat. I was learning all this, wondering which type of skiing I should have tried first. But it wasn't a choice. This expedition required cross-country skis.*

We set off the following morning to celebrate National Day in bright sunshine.

'There's no rush, we can take our time getting to the top,' someone called out.

This was maybe a small concession to me and my inexperience. Everyone was wearing their rucksacks with small Norwegian flags sticking out of them. Now I understood why everyone had looked strangely at my suitcase. As I'd no idea what might be needed on this trip, I took nothing. I was happy about that. The prospect of hauling myself up a hill was burden enough without an additional one on my back.

The first part was flattish so skiing was okay, not easy but manageable. I should have enjoyed the view, but I had to give most of my attention to the two metres of snow in front of the skis. Balance, push and glide, use the poles, alternate arms and feet, get a good rhythm, get a good rhythm. My mantra. The theory was easy. The sweat flowed. The pace wasn't slow in spite of the initial 'no rush' comment.

'God, I'm glad they didn't say time was tight!'

I was finding and using muscles that appeared to have been dormant for the previous three decades.

'You feeling alright back there?'

'Yes, sure. Not the easiest thing I've ever done but I'm with you.'

I could say nothing else to these kind hosts, not wanting them to think I was incapable of learning. While the energy required for skiing on the flat isn't huge, the nervous energy of a new skier is enormous. 'Relax' is a word that disappears from the vocabulary even though you know no progress can be made with every muscle and sinew as taut and tight as a steel rope. After half an hour, just when I thought I was feeling a little more in control, the gradient changed.

'Bit of a climb here. Doesn't go on for long, then there's a super down.'

My heart was somewhere in the region of my rubber boots. While the Norwegians always say that there is no shame in turning and not reaching one's target, they use this expression to convince people the weather is boss and no one should continue in dangerous conditions. As the sun was shining and the day was clear, I didn't think I could invoke this. So onwards it was. This is where 'herring-boning' comes into play. Peter said real experts run up hills, keeping their weight well forward and angling the skis outwards at the tips. This is the herring-bone shape. Lesser folk do the same but go slowly. In my case, it was a plod. Getting the weight in the right place is critical or you fall and slide back.

'Shit, shit, shit, shit, shit.'

I discovered where my weight shouldn't be. Although I'd fallen on the previous day, getting up on the flat was much easier than getting up on a slope. And this was my first slope. Cross-country skis are long, and although the heel is free and allows bending and kneeling, the skis get in the way. Which technique to choose was the problem. To kneel then try to stand? To keep the skis apart or together? To use the poles or not? While I was having

23

*this philosophical discussion with myself, Peter came back.
'Get your skis across the slope, then sit still for a few moments to get your breath back.'*

*I did as I was told, the best advice being the bit about the breath as by this time I was panting like a dog, flushed and sweating.
'Should have brought a spare T-shirt with me. That's something I've learned.'*

With the aid of a pole from Peter to hang on to, and pushing on one of mine, I managed to lever myself upright. Manoeuvring back into the herring-bone position was another struggle but eventually I was able to set off again. The rest of the group were out of sight so there was pressure to increase the speed. Just two falls later, somewhat easier to recover from than the first, I reached the top of the rise where the others had waited. They sat in the sunshine, relaxed, chatting, totally at home in their environment. None of them looked as if they had exerted themselves at all.

'Will I ever be able to enjoy skiing like that?' I wondered. 'Yes, of course I will,' said the whip-cracker within me. 'Don't give up!'

They were all getting ready to move on. The problem with being the slowest in any group is that you never get much recovery time; everyone is ready to set off again as soon as you arrive. This wasn't the last time I experienced this phenomenon.

'Right, we've got a nice run down now, not too steep. There is a bend part way down so you'll need to snowplough to control your speed and then another just before it flattens out again. You can take that one as fast as you like as there's a good run out at the end.'

I heard the words. No doubt they were sensible instructions.

I would snowplough if I had the first idea what to

do. Am I going to be going fast enough to need to control my speed? Don't like the idea of the bends. These thoughts went through my head as I watched the others depart one after the other. It looked so simple. They just stood on their skis, gave a small push with both poles and slid down the slope. So, when my turn came, I did the same. The first few metres were great. There's a wonderful freedom that goes with skis sliding over snow, with no effort required. However, before I had time to think, I was lying in the snow, probably a better outcome than getting totally out of control with all the potential consequences. Good old Peter was herring-boning back up the hill to give me the required snowploughing lesson.

'Tips together, rather like a reverse herringbone, and bend your knees.'

'I've got it! Fantastic!'

By the end of the slope, having fallen at both bends, I had more or less mastered the rudiments of coming downhill. From there to the top of the hill was an undulating track but nothing as severe as the slope already conquered. I felt totally exhausted but was encouraged by the sight of the emerging celebrations. I'd assumed that the various rucksacks carried spare clothing and other ski-related stuff. Not so. A bottle of Martini appeared, together with gin, cocktail cherries, cocktail sticks and glasses. These were real glasses, made of glass, not plastic. Of course, everything was intact; a breakage wasn't a possibility. The toast to 'Syttende mai'– 17th May – had to be done properly.

'Gratulerer med Dagen!'

'Congratulations!'

'Cheers!'

'Skål!'

And so I sat and enjoyed the company of these new friends and basked in the glow of the achievement of having

25

got there, not skilfully or with style, but with Norwegians in the Norwegian way. The bug had bitten and I was now a committed cross-country ski enthusiast. It would be good to end the story there, but of course, the party had to return to the hytte. As I'd made it to the top, the Norwegians assumed a level of competence that didn't exist and at the appropriate time, just set off with some speed, their national flags fluttering behind them, a spectacle I would long remember. None of them had actually seen me ski more than a few metres as I was at the end of the line. The celebratory alcohol I'd consumed helped to soften the pain of the return journey. I got back, all focus being on a hot shower, an early bed and deep, comforting sleep.

On this day, however, no one was allowed an early night. I was persuaded to go to a nightclub, anything other than enthusiasm being unacceptable to my hosts. That such a place should exist in Finse was a surprise, but it did; the town boasted one. I'm no expert on nightclubs, usually regarding them as someone else's overpriced entertainment, so this was another learning experience. We arrived to find a queue outside the building; all the best places in Norway have a queue. At minus fourteen degrees, you really have to want to go in to justify hanging around. The inside warmth was welcoming and everyone progressed to the bar. I thought it odd that no one bought me a drink but when I realised how much a beer cost, the reason became clear. No one buys rounds here. I bought my own, fatigue blurring the pain of the outlay. Norway was living up to its reputation for being an expensive country.

'Are you having a good time? Did you enjoy today? You look a bit tired.'

Our host separated himself from the bar long enough to talk to me.

'Yes, I've really enjoyed myself. But I'm not a bit tired. I'm totally exhausted.'

26

Peter woke me up in time to take me back to the hytte.

Ski Tips

It was May and the snow had disappeared in Oslo, so Tony wasn't able to continue his skiing career there. Nevertheless, when we arrived, he was our expert. He couldn't wait to buy equipment and plan for the winter. One evening, he returned home from work carrying an armful of kit.

'Look what I've bought!'

He triumphantly displayed three pairs of cross-country skis for the children, together with boots and poles. There was a vibrant second-hand market amongst Tony's colleagues and he had jumped in. It seemed no one bought new for kids so we followed suit. This wasn't because we feared they might not enjoy the sport – Tony didn't even consider such a possibility – but just because they were all still growing and it was a sensible, cheap option. Cross-country skiing is done by everyone in Norway throughout their lives. At school, it's the equivalent of running in England and everyone is expected to take part and have their own gear. No one hired anything; there were no local shops in the ski hire business. So we were simply Norwegianising our family.

But that wasn't the whole ski story. We had the other type of skiing to consider. If Tony was our expert for cross-country equipment, we had no one with any downhill skiing knowledge. We had, at least, learned we needed two separate sets of equipment. Again, we turned successfully to the second-hand market to equip the children. For ourselves, long past the growing stage, we went for new. Sales were on in Oslo and there were bargains about so we decided we should buy then, both for cross-country and downhill, rather than wait until the winter when we'd have to pay full price for the new season's wares. I have never spent so much money on something I knew nothing about. There were a few basic rules regarding length of skis relative to height so we dutifully followed those. Otherwise, we were at the mercy of the salespeople. At least they spoke English.

'What size shoe do you take?'

'English size 4. That's 37, I think.'

'You have narrow feet. These should fit perfectly.'

I was presented with a grey boot, hard and stiff with four clips across the front. The assistant opened it up for me and levered my foot into it.

'Bang your heel on the floor to get it completely back in the boot.'

I did as I was told. Click, click, click, click and my foot was imprisoned. He did the same for the other foot.

'Is that comfortable?'

'No.'

'Well, you need to walk around for a while to get the plastic of the boot warmed up then it will soften and feel better.'

So I walked around the shop feeling like a robot and wondering how 'comfortable' and 'ski boot' could ever form part of the same sentence. Cross-country skiing was becoming more appealing. At least the boots were manageable. After half an hour, during which time Tony also acquired some boots, I decided nothing was changing so it was decision time. I was feeling embarrassed about how long this purchase was taking.

'Do they feel better now?'

'No.'

'Not at all? What's the problem?'

'They feel too tight.'

'Can you move your toes?'

'Yes. They aren't squashed. My feet just feel too encased.'

'But that's how you need to feel. You need a snug fit to be able to control the skis. How much skiing have you done?'

'None. I'm a beginner.'

'Ah, that explains it.'

So I bought the boots, feeling that it was my inexperience making them feel wrong. Two years later, I bought new ones. The original pair was never comfortable. I had frequent pins and needles in my feet and the boots were so difficult to put on and take off that once I had them on, they had to stay there until the end of the day. Maybe the guy in the shop saw a sucker coming when I turned up. I do have narrow feet so if they were too tight for me, I can't think who they would have fitted. And the moral of the story? Try on lots of pairs from a store you know and trust. And walk about in them for ages. Embarrassment over the time it takes is irrelevant. Shops know the process.

We also needed clothing. Again, a kindly sales assistant pointed us towards one-piece suits for the children. These, apparently, were what all children wore in the winter, not just for skiing but also for going to school and general outdoor activities. They were uni-sex, so I thought they'd get plenty of use within the family. We acquired three sales bargains and the children loved them. Goggles, gloves and hats completed the purchases. They were now fully equipped. As soon as we got back to the house everything had to be tried on.

'Can we put the skis on as well?'

'Not in the house. You might damage the floor.'

'Well, can we go outside?'

'There's nowhere to ski.'

'That doesn't matter. We can pretend.'

We caused much amusement to the neighbours when three children clad in ski suits, ski boots, woolly hats, gloves and goggles, brandishing ski poles, emerged through the front door to parade about on the grass wearing their skis. The sun was shining and the temperature was twenty-five degrees. The fact that no one walks on grass wearing skis for fear of damaging the bases was a refinement we had yet to discover. In a way, it introduced us to the locals, and from then on, we would get small children coming to the door and asking, (in Norwegian, of course), 'Are the English coming out?'

We had been identified.

It seemed a long time to the children but snow eventually arrived. We had a light covering in Oslo, but had heard that there was enough snow for cross-country skiing a couple of hours away at Norefjell in the mountains. It was November, too early for most Norwegians to be out on skis, but we were tempted. A phone call from Keith, an English friend, sealed it.

'We thought we'd go for a trip on Saturday. Do you fancy coming along? Marit can help you a bit.'

Marit was his Norwegian girlfriend, a good cross-country skier, so it seemed ideal. The children were definitely up for it. At five, seven and nine, you just assume you'll be able to ski. We arrived at the starting place. The snow was disappointing, thinner than we'd expected with tree roots and stones sticking out. The trail ran through the trees and was a 'marked trail', normally prepared by a special machine that cuts beautiful parallel grooves for the skis to glide in. However, it was too early in the season for that.

'Not ideal conditions,' said Marit, 'but we'll

31

manage.'

She and Keith proceeded to wax their skis, rubbing hard, coloured stuff in little squat cylinders on the bases and polishing them afterwards with a block of cork. It was akin to black magic for us. Then they set off to have a look around. We had no wax so were able to skip that part of the proceedings.

'What's the best way to do this? Should we put our skis on first, then do the kids, or the reverse?'

'I think it's best to sort the kids out. Once we have skis on, it'll be more difficult to move.'

That was a true statement. We put their skis on, not a difficult process, and told them to stand still while we sorted ours out. How many children stand still when told to? Within seconds, Joe was trying to go downhill and immediately sat down; as the oldest, he felt he should show the way. Anna tried to turn round and got her skis either side of a tree. Tim, our youngest, had stayed still, something he rarely did, and fell over on the spot. At this point, Tony had one ski on and I was still on feet only, so I went to the rescue. Joe was on a slope so I had no idea what to do with him.

'You'll just have to wait for Daddy. He'll sort you out.'

I managed to drag Anna backwards so she was away from the tree and pointing in the right direction and I stood Tim up.

'Now, please, don't move. Give us chance to get our skis on, too.'

It was unlikely I'd be able to do better with my skis on when my attempts to help had so far been minimal, but I had no choice. Tony had his on and had reached Joe who was now more or less vertical. At this point, Marit returned. I took her smile to be sympathy rather than amused incredulity.

32

'If you just get down this little slope, it's pretty flat and a good place to practise. I'll help you there.'

I nodded. The little slope looked steep to me. We all tried to do as Marit said but made the fundamental error of being too close together. Joe and Tim ended up in a heap demonstrating the domino effect. Anna, who seemed inexplicably fond of trees, got herself into another positional problem. She and I were pointing in opposite directions, one on each side of the track.

'Mummy, I'm stuck.'

'Anna, so am I.'

I tried to turn round but the path wasn't wide enough and I wasn't sufficiently competent. This was ceasing to be fun; no, it had not even started to be fun. Only in retrospect could I see the funny side of it. Tony was managing better – he had done it before, after all – and sorted Anna out. We stayed there about an hour. I never got down the slope to the easy area. I'd stopped believing easy areas existed, anyway. The children managed better than I did. Falling over came more naturally to them and they were nearer the ground, so their level of frustration was lower. Marit had a look of disbelief on her face.

'I've never come so far to ski so little,' was her only comment.

We returned home. I'd used an enormous amount of energy going nowhere. Fortunately, no one offered me any money for my skis the following day or I would have sold them. I'd have paid someone to take them away.

By Christmas, we had proper snow in Oslo. The Norefjell memory faded and we discovered the blind trail. This is a fairly flat loop where blind skiers are taught, about as easy to manage as possible. When I first learned that blind people ski, I was speechless with admiration. Learning is bad enough with good sight. I discovered waxing and suddenly, with proper wax, good conditions and no

33

gradient, I was able to move forward without falling. It was a Eureka moment. It felt good although it probably didn't look great. We progressed to the golf course, another beginners' area, and started to feel more competent. I don't play golf; the nearest I've ever got to a green is skiing over it. But I appreciated this course. The children all skied at school and we became addicts of the trails in Nordmarka, the area to the north of Oslo. This is possibly the best terrain in the world for cross-country skiing, kilometre after kilometre of intertwining trails. We were often passed by gentlemen in their seventies skiing with their grandchildren – rather deflating the confidence, but what the hell, we were enjoying it. We looked out for King Olav who frequently skied in the area with his companion and dog but never saw him. Well, he might have gone by while we were concentrating as there was never much time for anything else.

We also discovered skiing by moonlight. There are many lighted trails in the Oslo area, necessary because of the shortness of the days in winter when it can be dark before four o'clock in the afternoon. We often went out in the early evening for a lap or two of the nearest five-kilometre lighted loop, less than half an hour away. Always well lit, when the moon was visible, it was really bright, the heavily laden branches of the pine trees bending low with sparkling snow crystals and the neatly cut tracks showing the way ahead. These trails were well used but you could still find yourself alone along a stretch of the route. You could believe that you were the only people in existence, still, silent and romantic. We loved it.

We thought it the most beautiful place in the world.

Our enthusiasm took us out on evenings when the Norwegians stayed in. This happened when it hadn't snowed for a while and the surface was hard-packed and icy. Such conditions require skill, more skill than we had.

On one memorable evening, I took a heavy fall, landing on my left side. It was painful but we had to continue as going back was no quicker. I proceeded to fall several more times and I always fall in the same way. What began as a small bruise became bigger until all the outside of my thigh felt sore and swollen. For cross-country skiing, thick clothing isn't necessary as you generate so much heat through exercise. It does mean, however, there isn't much protection when you take a tumble. The cold had somewhat anaesthetised me so it was a shock when I got home.

'Come and have a look at my leg!'

Tony was aghast. I had a deep purple bruise about twenty centimetres in diameter. Although he was sympathetic, his first reaction was to grab the camera.

'We have to record this! There may never be such a superb specimen again. Just hope we can get it printed and it isn't considered to be obscene photography!'

I still have the photograph. Tony was right; I've never had another bruise like it.

So much for the thin cross-country skis. Although we were learning to love them, we all wanted to try 'proper' skiing, the downhill or alpine variety. We got out the map and decided that a weekend in Geilo would be the best bet. This was a four-hour drive from Oslo and was a small but popular resort. We booked a self-catering cabin – a hytte – and set off with our equipment on a Friday evening as soon as the children were home from school. We listened to tapes on the way. 'Gobelino, the witch's cat' was a favourite. Anything to make the journey go quickly. The hytte was cosy and comfortable and the whole thing had an air of adventure. The children went to bed, eventually, in a high state of expectation.

The first adventure was the following morning, but it wasn't on skis. Our hytte, while well-equipped in many ways, did not have a bathroom or loo. The six cabins all shared a toilet block about fifty metres away. I grabbed my towel and wash bag and rushed out early, the plentiful coffee of the previous evening making itself felt. I promptly fell over on the sheet ice close to our door. Everywhere seemed far icier than when we arrived. I managed to stand up but two more paces brought me to my knees again. I really did need the loo so I was reluctant to return. Progress in a vertical position seemed impossible and I didn't want to do any damage before actually reaching the slopes. The only way forward was to spread my towel in front of me and crawl over it. I then replaced it in front of me and crawled further. In this pathetic manner, I arrived at the toilet block. The towel had very few dry spots on it so washing was rudimentary. The relief once I'd got there was, however, both physically and psychologically immense. Returning followed a similar pattern, my progress being faster as I mastered the towel-crawling technique. Maybe I could invent a new sport. I saw no one on my journey although I wondered how many I amused behind their curtains.

After the fiasco on cross-country skis, we decided a proper lesson would be the best way to start. Tony had booked us a family session with a local instructor. We met by the appointed T-bar lift at nine o'clock. I wondered where the lesson would be. In front of us was a steep slope with people skiing down. Some looked a bit wobbly but they could all do it after a fashion. Einar introduced himself.

'We'll practise a bit down here first. You need to walk up the hill sideways, then we can ski down in a snowplough.'

We all managed that. So he got us to walk up a bit higher. On my third attempt, I gathered some speed and found myself heading for the lift queue.

'Turn! Turn!' yelled Einar, forgetting he had not yet taught me how to do anything but go straight.

The inevitable happened and I skied straight into the ski queue, knocking people over like skittles and falling over myself. I got my skis tangled up with various other bits of equipment and bodies and had to be extracted by Einar. He said nothing. He just looked at me. Meanwhile, Tim had fallen and hurt his knee. One of the kind ladies in the kiosk asked him in for sympathy and chocolate and this seemed the best option. He retired from the lesson.

'Right. We'll go up in the lift now and ski down the whole of the beginners' slope.'

This was the beginners' slope? All of it? This mountain with people who could ski? I couldn't think too much about it as we were getting our instructions.

'I'll take Anna and Joe up with me. Anna can stand in front of my legs and Joe can stand beside me. You two can follow on the T-bar behind. Just watch how I catch it and do the same.'

He manoeuvred the two children into position, half turned, grabbed the bar of the T as it came round and pulled it down behind him so that it was just under Joe's bottom and partway across his thighs. It was an easy, slick movement he had done hundreds, probably thousands, of times. We shuffled ourselves forward and realised we were too slow to get into position for the next T-bar. No matter, we let it pass us by. I stood on the inside, Tony on the outside and we both reached up to grab the T. We touched it but it sailed past.

'Hold tighter next time and pull.'

'Okay.'

As we tried to get up from the snow where the next bar had propelled us, the following T-bar sailed on. Getting up was no easy matter but we eventually got there. The length of the queue was becoming an embarrassment. Einar arrived with both children. In the time it had taken us to fail to get on the T-bar, he had ridden to the top and brought both children down. He deposited the children and told them to practise at the bottom. Grabbing my arm, he slid alongside me, shouting to Tony that he would be back. The T-bar did everything he asked of it and we got to the top, my legs stiff and tense, my heart thumping and my stomach somersaulting. The prospect of having to get down the slope was making me feel sick and my legs were trembling. All strength had gone. I think Einar sensed this as he pushed my skis into a 'V' shape with the tips together and skied down the hill backwards, hanging onto them. I just fell in love with him. Anyone who could do that was a hero in my eyes. Tony didn't need so much help and by the time he got down, our lesson was over.

We then had to decide how to progress. Geilo has two separate parts to it and we decided that the other, smaller side, called Vestlia, might be better for us with fewer people. We went there after lunch. The temperature was dropping and we were worried about the children getting too cold. So we told them to wait at the bottom of the lift while we both went up to see what it was like. The ski map indicated that one of the runs from the top was a blue and we were hoping that would suit us.

To start with, however, we had to negotiate our first drag lift, usually called a Poma in Norway after the manufacturer. This is a steel pole with a round disc at the end. The technique is to grab the pole as it moves past and slip the disc between the legs. You don't sit on it, just lean against it and if you keep your skis parallel, you get dragged up the mountain. I know all the details now. On our first day, we stood and watched a few people then joined the queue. It was easier than the T-bar as you only had yourself to think about. Everyone rode the lift alone. Tony went up first and I followed, hanging on with all my strength. I was feeling proud of myself as I'd caught the Poma at the first attempt. The track upwards was icy and far bumpier than the T-bar track. My skis were sliding about and, I suppose inevitably, I fell. I was still holding on and found myself being dragged up on my back, hanging on by one hand. I had no idea how long it took to get to the top but thought that any means of getting there was better than being stranded part way up. Then one ski hit a bump and came off. I let go as I didn't want to lose it. I don't think my arm would have let me hang on much longer anyway. Someone on a lower Poma managed to rescue my ski and dropped it by me as I lay in the snow. At least that was one problem solved.

    To the right of me were trees. I couldn't see a piste and didn't fancy my chances there. To my left, the area was more open so I set out in that direction. To say I was scared would be more than an understatement, but I didn't have much choice. I was on my own with no possibility of contacting anyone. What a luxury mobile phones are now! We always carry them; we even switch them on. But our early skiing days were pre-mobile phones. I managed to walk with one ski on, carrying the other like a cross between a walking stick and a crutch. The snow was deep and had come over the top of my boot. Even the tight fit could not prevent some sliding inside and melting. It wasn't my major worry at that moment. I reached what appeared to be a piste. However, the surface was nothing like the only piste I'd experienced, the beginners' slope. There were large piles of snow everywhere, with icy boulders scattered about. This was a lunar landscape. Fortunately, the part I'd arrived at wasn't too steep and I managed to put my second ski back on and attempted to snowplough. But it was useless, I could make little progress, there were too many obstacles, lumps of ice, mounds of snow. My legs were shaking, the uncontrollable shaking that comes with attempting something physical that is too difficult. Although hoping someone would come along and help me, I was beginning to realise there was nobody else around. Where were the skiers? The slope was deserted. I sat down, or rather slithered into a sitting position. Realising the impossibility of ever getting down on my skis, I removed them. Carrying skis and poles when close to tears, freezing cold, none too steady on my feet and basically lost isn't an experience I want to repeat. Time was moving on. It would be dark before long. After something like ten hours, (well, it felt like it), I heard the noise of a motor. A guy on a skidoo drove down the slope towards me.

'What are you doing here? This slope is closed. Its condition isn't good enough for skiing. And it's a black, not suitable for a beginner.'

That explained a lot. I told my sad tale. The guy just looked exasperated and told me to sit behind him. He strapped my skis on the back and set off with a roar. I'd not been ready for the acceleration and fell off the seat into the small trailer attached to the skidoo. In this undignified and uncomfortable way, on my back, legs in the air, I reached the bottom of the slope and the rest of the family.

Tony had put out an alert after he'd reached the top of the lift, skied down the blue slope and failed to find me. Someone had seen me fall off so a rescue party set out to find me. The children were fed up and hungry, Tony was relieved, I was frustrated, annoyed, bruised, cold, tearful and a host of other adjectives. That was the end of our first day of alpine skiing. When I think back, it's amazing I ever continued. Had it been just a week's ski holiday, it may have been my only attempt at the sport. But we had bought the equipment; we were living in Norway where the winters are long and hard if you don't enjoy them. And to enjoy them, you have to ski. Tony was his usual optimistic self, so I had to contend with that too. He'd enjoyed himself until I disappeared, so stopping wasn't an option. We went back to the hytte for a hot meal and a discussion on the best strategy for the following day.

Keener and Better

How did we get from bumbling, inept beginners to practised ski bums? The key was living for five years in Norway. Where skiing is concerned, you either give up and begin knitting or give yourself over to it completely. I did knit, a particularly Norwegian activity, but it was secondary. We went away most weekends to the mountains, either Geilo where we'd started or Hemsedal, a slightly bigger resort with its own challenges. We met other Brits also trying to learn so we had someone else to complain to about our bruises and inadequacies. We also met Anne-Berit and Chris, a Norwegian-English couple who were not only good skiers but ex-ski instructors. We became friends, skied with them often and learned by copying. Learning as a thirty-something is vastly different from starting as a child. Anne-Berit had first put skis on at the age of two. Our kids, although older than she'd been, learned at the right age. Tim can't remember learning to ski; I don't think I could ever forget. It didn't take him long to work out who was the best person to follow. He became Anne-Berit's shadow. We progressed rapidly from

'Stay behind Mummy and Daddy. Turn where we turn. Don't go too fast!'

to

'See you at the bottom. Wait for us before going back up.'

The children were more confident than we were although none of us would have won prizes for style. Giant snowploughs and the lavatory position were effective, safe and the modus operandi of all three younger members of the family. Lifts were the main issue. Lots of T-bars and drag lifts; chairs were far rarer in those days. The kids couldn't manage them on their own, so we were needed. Tony rode T-bars bent almost double with the crossbar of the T behind his knees in order to get Tim up. Drag lifts were single-person, so although we could help them to get on, they were then on their own. Whenever a lift stopped, we wondered which of our children had fallen off. This happened often in our first season. Because of a lift incident, Anna was the first in the family to ski the hardest run in Hemsedal, a black, and one we had no intention of going near. The lift that ran alongside it also served easier slopes. We'd all gone up several times and skied back down a blue. We tended to get spread out but gathered together at the bottom of the piste. On one occasion, we realised we were one short.

'Where's Anna?'

'She went up. She must have fallen somewhere. Hope she's alright.'

Tony took the lift back up to look for her while I stayed at the bottom in case she appeared. Skiing is a dangerous sport and all sorts of dreadful scenarios were flashing through my mind. I waited. Eventually, Tony reappeared having retraced our route and not found her. While Hemsedal is small as ski resorts go, there's a lot of it when you've lost a seven-year-old child. There were wooded parts of the mountain between the slopes, plenty of places where an injured child could be trapped and hidden. Panic was beginning to rise and I was contemplating alerting the ski patrol when we spotted a small figure clad in a red one-piece suit high up on the black slope. It traversed in a wide snowplough across the slope to the far edge, turned, and then repeated the manoeuvre.

'Is it Anna?'

'It might be. Too far away to tell.'

'If it is, she's skiing the black.'

The four of us watched as, in total control, this little person made its way down an otherwise empty slope. After a while, we realised it was Anna. Immense relief, although I was still worried that she'd make it in one piece. I ran up to her as she reached the bottom and hugged her. She burst into tears.

'What happened, darling? Where were you?'

No reply.

'Did you fall off the lift? Do you know you've just skied down the black? You did so well to get down. None of us has done it.'

Anna's philosophy was always to ignore anything she'd done that was either naughty or somewhat dubious on the grounds that if you didn't talk about it, it hadn't happened. This came into the 'ignore it' category' in her mind, even though she'd done nothing wrong. We never discovered what happened, but deduced she'd fallen off the lift near the top, had made her way to the only slope accessible at that point and skied down it. It happened to be the black.

One day after we'd been skiing with Anne-Berit, she stopped and watched Tim go down the slope ahead of her.

'You should get him into racing, you know.'

The children were now all skiing well although racing was a new concept to us all. Norway is a land of sports clubs. Most people belong to one, often as a family group, so I decided we should do the same to give the kids racing opportunities. Out of my comfort zone and still with piecemeal, halting Norwegian (although, being stubborn, I would not resort to English), I phoned round some local clubs. I can't say many were enthralled at the prospect of three English kids joining their racing groups. But I prevailed and we were welcomed by a club called Fossum. Lots of children race and there is a programme of events for all ages. We were sucked in. Joe found it hard to accept that his brother, four years younger, was turning into a better racer than he was. We all have our strengths and Tim was finding his. He was selected to join an elite children's race group, *Alpin Ung*. He loved it. His Norwegian wasn't good and although he had a fine vocabulary of skiing terms, simple Norwegian sometimes defeated him.

'Mum, something's happening on Wednesday, but I don't know what it is.'

We sorted it out. At least he understood the days of the week. Ski racing became a significant part of our lives and activities at Fossum important. In our last winter in Norway, the club invited everyone to a fun weekend in Geilo. We saw skiing in yet another light. The men of the group set about building a bar out of snow at the bottom of the slope and served smoked salmon and *gløgg*, the Norwegian version of mulled wine. I had never before mixed skiing and alcohol. We considered it rather like drinking and driving, although I've since learned the error of my ways and a vin chaud is now an essential part of the day. A music system was set up and the kids performed a wonderful routine to Michael Jackson's 'Bad', keeping in time with each other by means of Walkmans wired under their ski helmets. The wine and the atmosphere were relaxing me beautifully; I should have known it wouldn't last.

I didn't mind joining in the racing – all parents had to do the same as the kids – even though I came last. However, when it came to skiing to music, dancing in effect, I was about as bad as it's possible to be. There was no escape. One of the coaches showed us some moves but I had neither the balance nor the skill to perform them. I'm not particularly flexible and the many layers of clothing made things worse. Not wanting to fall, I resorted to bending my knees rapidly up and down like a demented chicken and waving my arms around. It was over in a matter of minutes and I hastened off the slope to receive the scorn of my children. I'd not appreciated that one of the guys was videoing the whole event and I had to undergo the extreme embarrassment of watching my dreadful performance later that evening, along with everyone else. To make matters worse, everyone was awarded a prize. I hope that most people were sufficiently inebriated to forget how awful the whole thing was. It still haunts me now.

Our cross-country skiing, against all odds, also improved. The Norwegians love to race and there are many events open to skiers of all abilities. Tony would go out training with Chris, an accomplished cross-country skier, to prepare for taking part in the Holmenkollen ski marathon, a full forty-two kilometres. This is an annual race, open to all, which finishes near the famous Holmenkollen ski jump in Oslo. It's timed to coincide with one of the major ski jumping competitions which means all marathon competitors arrive into a packed stadium, the home run being directly in front of the ski jump. I was also tempted to do the race, and a good Norwegian girlfriend, Torill, took responsibility for getting me into shape. We skied every Wednesday morning and always had wonderful weather. We were so lucky that 'real Wednesday weather' became a synonym for sunshine and good snow. Torill was an unusual Norwegian in that she didn't speak perfect English. Part of the Wednesday exercise was also language training. We would speak English on the way out and when we changed direction to return, we changed languages and I got some Norwegian practice. No one believed we'd be able to do this, but we did. So both the speaking and the skiing improved.

Torill and Chris, our coaches, had both competed in the Holmenkollen race on several occasions previously so were able to advise us. One of the key factors was waxing the skis. It all depends on temperature. Really cold weather is easy to cope with and the choice of which wax to use a simple one. As the temperature rises towards zero, it becomes more complex. For relative novices like us, it was a minefield. For our first race, the conditions were warmer than ideal.

'You can wax your own skis.'

Tony normally prepared all our skis but this time it was to be my own responsibility.

'I'm not being blamed for the wrong wax when you have problems part way round the course. You choose your wax, you put it on, you manage the consequences. I'll do my own. We then can only blame – or congratulate – ourselves.'

Around zero, the wrong wax will result either in no grip, which you need in order to go uphill, or sticking to the snow with consequent absence of glide. No grip means sliding around, wasted energy and lack of rhythm. Sticking means the snow builds up on the base of the skis and has to be scraped off. Neither is good. Both result in frustrated, slow skiers. We watched the weather forecast anxiously and left the waxing until the last possible moment when the information was most reliable.

We knew that applying lots of thin layers of wax, rubbing the skis with the cork polisher between applications, was the recommended technique. We each chose slightly different combinations of colours, the colours signifying suitability for different ranges of temperature. It was a black art, extremely black in our hands, neither of us saying exactly what we were using, nor how many layers we were applying. We spent hours on the skis, a job usually taking several minutes. It all added to the build-up for the

47

race.

One wax we both wanted to avoid was something called *klister*. It comes in a tube, unlike the hard waxes mostly used, as it is sticky and is only used above zero degrees. It even sounds sticky. It is horrible to apply and gets everywhere. It does when I use it, anyway. Popular opinion said the weather would be just cold enough for it not to be necessary. I decided to take some with me, just in case, as re-waxing at some point would be necessary in a race of that length. Getting cold klister out of the tube and spreading it evenly is difficult, so I decided to keep it in my jacket pocket. My body warmth would be enough to soften it sufficiently for use. Tony put his in a small rucksack. Well, if he wanted to struggle with a solid tube, that was his affair. I was doing my own thing.

The race was divided into waves, the elite group going first and then others according to anticipated speed, just like running marathons. We all went by bus to the start at our appointed times. The atmosphere was incredible, like nothing I had previously experienced, a mixture of camaraderie, competition and liniment. It was fortunate there were many portaloos as the combination of nerves and cold meant everyone was running. I was one of hundreds yet felt special to be taking part in the race. I looked round at the crowd of skiers in my wave. Most were Norwegian, probably experienced and doing it for the tenth or fifteenth time. Many were older than me, not surprising as my anticipated time was far slower than for most women of my age. Torill was in a wave far ahead of me. We lined up across a huge field and set off at a klaxon. The group rapidly spread forward so that we formed an ever-narrowing file of skiers trying not to trip each other up. I had a dread of falling and being skied into the ground so was glad to let folk go past. At the first bend, there was a band playing and a group of people cheering. I felt hugely motivated by this.

People were cheering me on – me, an English woman who was no expert! The whole race was punctuated with bands, food stations and flag-waving groups, especially as we got closer to Oslo, making the race easier than I could have imagined. I knew it was important to take on food and drink so dutifully stopped at each food station. It wasn't a hardship – the goods on offer were tasty.

Around half way, my skis were slipping so I decided to re-wax. Klister or hard wax? The decision was made for me. The tube in my pocket had warmed up as anticipated but had also split. I'd had a tumble on a steep downhill and the tube was firmly glued to the interior of my pocket. No way could I use it and I had the additional problem of trying to de-klister the hand that had sought out the tube. I just zipped up the pocket for later investigation and did my best in the loo with my hand. My best was poor so I had to replace my glove over the sticky mess, ruining the interior of my glove as well. All was forgotten as I approached the Holmenkollen stadium. The noise of the crowd reached back along the trail and encouraged the weary skiers to complete the last few kilometres. As I came within sight of the finish line, an excellent Norwegian ski jumper landed. So I finished the race with the roar of the crowd around my ears, excited people jumping up and down and waving Norwegian flags. I knew it wasn't for me but I experienced what a race winner must feel like. Fortunately, I managed the last stretch without stumbling.

As for my jacket, I had to cut the pocket out and sew up the zip. I threw the gloves away.

***

When the time came to leave Norway, nobody was keen. There was a lot to miss but I set about finding activities for everyone to take part in back in England. Tim

49

was being difficult.

'There are swimming lessons, Cubs, drama classes, gym, trampolining – what do you fancy doing?'

'Skiing.'

'Come on, you know it's not Norway. How can you ski here?'

He could, of course, and we discovered dry slope racing. Anna and Tim raced with Sandown Ski Club (Joe opted for Drama club). Our weekends were taken up with trips round the country to various slopes, and there was a fair measure of success in the races. Tony and I became useful amateur officials, gatekeeping being the main task. It is unexpectedly tiring standing sideways on a slope looking at a few poles to make sure no racers straddle them. A straddle, when one ski passes either side of the pole instead of both on the same side, results in disqualification. Sometimes we would drive hundreds of miles to see either Tim or Anna straddle at the first gate. There was compensation, though, when they won. The kids learned a lot of technique on the artificial slopes but they were not an end in themselves, or at least, not for this family.

Snow called and the kids went on training and racing camps in the snow with either Sandown or the Downhill Only Club, a long-standing club set up many years ago by Brits in Switzerland. They were both selected for the English Alpine Team and Tim went on to be a member of the British Team, becoming British Junior Champion several times. A large amount of our income was diverted into skiing. We were frequent camp followers for Tim, giving us plenty of opportunity to ski in a variety of resorts. I never got used to the nerves associated with watching a son compete in an important race, or in any race, really. But that's another story.

All this involvement with skiing meant it remained an important part of our lives back in England, not something we'd left behind in Norway. Skiing every year for two to three weeks prevented us from losing our skills although that was about it. There was no improvement. We discovered good and bad ski resorts, useful knowledge when later we decided to buy a place in the Alps

But what about cross-country skiing? That was harder to keep going outside Scandinavia. Prepared trails exist in France, sometimes good ones, but they are poor competition for the kilometres of prepared piste on offer to alpine skiers. We'd become reasonably competent in Norway, to our own surprise. Back in England, there was little in the way of cross-country skiing substitute. We had, bravely or foolishly, bought ourselves some roller skis in Norway. These are shorter than snow skis, with wheels at each end and are for use on tarmac. You can't snowplough on them so there is no way of slowing down. You need to leave your brain behind as no amateur in their right mind goes near them. Serious racers use them for training but ours have spent most of their life in a cupboard. On their occasional outings, they have caused badly grazed knees, bruised hips and incredulous looks. In anticipation of being able to continue our Holmenkollen racing careers, we began running on a regular basis, even doing the odd half-marathon. Norway certainly has a lot to answer for! We did manage to return and compete once more at Holmenkollen.

However, our first love is alpine skiing and so the plans began of one day having our own place in the French Alps where we could spend serious amounts of time. We made it happen. And now we were here, retired, accountable just to ourselves, with all the time in the world, beginning our second career as ski bums.

Skiing in our valley

It was too late to ski on the day we arrived, so we settled in and unpacked. The snow was high on our little terrace and there were swept piles in the car park. All good signs. We should have some excellent skiing conditions. Tony opened a bottle of Mondeuse, one of the best of the local red wines.

'Here's to our first day on the slopes as ski bums!'

The forecast was for sunshine the following day, minus ten degrees and a light breeze. It couldn't be better. We could see the lights of the piste machines twinkling high up the mountains as they did their nocturnal stints. What a strange life the pisteurs lead, barely seen workers converting the bumpy, much-skied slopes back into swathes of corduroy.

We were up early the following morning. Unknown to me, Tony had set the alarm for half past seven. On our body clocks, this was half past six.

'Did you mean to do that or was it an accident?'

'No accident. Can't miss good skiing time!'

We had all the time in the world but he couldn't break old habits. This wasn't the moment to protest about having a lie-in and, anyway, I wanted to get out early, too. The sky was clear and the first rays of sun were shining on Mont Vallon, the pointed mountain we can see from the apartment. Tony went out to get bread and provisions. It's cheese, ham and pâté for breakfast in France rather than our more customary cereal, jam and marmalade. We change eating habits as we change countries.

While Tony was out, I turned Radio Méribel on and waited for the snow and piste report.

Henry was there again with his avalanche warning. Not my favourite person. His advice is fine but I don't understand why an American has to give it. There are few Americans who ski in France. Nothing was going to annoy me today, though. Not only do you get the weather and snow report, there is usually a recommendation for a couple of pistes in the valley where the snow is particularly good. Today, Lagopède and Bartavelle were both *spécialement dammées*, specially prepared. We always listen out for this – it's a guaranteed wonderful beginning to the day.

We planned to be at the lifts when they opened, around nine o'clock. But first, we had to buy a season ticket for all of the three valleys – no self-respecting ski bum would ever buy a single valley pass. The price made our eyes water. Today, day one, we decided to stay in our valley and try to get our ski legs back before venturing further.

'What about Lagopède and Bartavelle?'

'Not Bartavelle, but we could try Lagopède.'

Bartavelle is a black slope. We like to try the blacks, to get out of our comfort zone, although survival is usually the best description of our efforts. We prefer them groomed, far easier than a bumpy, much-skied piste, so if one is recommended, we're there. But there's nothing like skiing a black badly to dent the confidence; it wouldn't be a good start to our first day.

I rushed down to the ski locker, as excited as the first time we ever skied there, especially as there was more snow than usual for early January. We then headed for the centre of Mottaret and the main lift stations. The chair lift, Combe, was running and there was no queue so we took it. It was cold. The wind stung our faces. We huddled together and pulled our neck pieces up over our mouths. From the top, we skied the short slope down to the nearby drag lift. Taking two exposed lifts, one after the other, was a bad idea but it was too late to change our minds. We could see Bartavelle alongside the lift, smooth and almost without skiers, a real temptation. Lagopède was just visible, looking equally good although busier. Common sense prevailed and we skied the red. It was a good recommendation. After a few runs there, Tony complained he'd got 'budgie feet'.

'I need to stop and take my boots off.'

We returned to Mottaret so we could take a cabin back up the mountain, a chance to sit down and for Tony to de-boot. I've never heard anyone else talk about 'budgie feet' but it perfectly describes the tense sensation both of us often experience on day one. We chose Plattières, a three-stage lift that gave us a good rest. From here we could see one of our favourite pistes, Mouflon. Today, we'd missed its first glory but it still looked good. Our confidence was rising. If you can't ski well on good snow in bright sunshine, you'll never ski well. We came down Mouflon with the old speed returning, no stops on the way, and a breathless exhilaration at the end.

'You know, you really should pull your trouser legs down. They don't look good at half-mast.'

'Oh God! The fashion police are here again. I thought they might not turn up this year.'

'They wouldn't if you pulled your trouser legs down.'

He indulged me and sorted his attire out. It was time for a vin chaud. It was well past time for a vin chaud. We'd been so involved in skiing that we could have missed it altogether. In our early skiing days in Norway, stops were strictly limited. Tony wouldn't stop until lunch, and then only for half an hour, although the children were allowed to go in for hot chocolate to keep warm. Age has mellowed him and he now agrees a break and a drink add to the pleasure of a holiday. The first day of the season deserved a morning reward.

We are now vin chaud experts. A good VC is one where you can actually detect some alcohol, it's not over-sweet and it's not bitter. It should also have some fruit in it – preferably a slice of orange. Some of the restaurants have a new trick: two sizes, a bit like pubs in England where you can have a medium or large glass of wine. The 'small' is the standard size served; it's enough for us. I frequently suffer from the well-known skiers' condition, 'vin chaud legs'; the one time I ordered the larger size, it brought on a severe attack. Revived, we had another ski down Mouflon into Mottaret and then went up the other, Courchevel, side of the valley.

Lunchtime took us to the Espace Confort near the bottom of Mont Vallon. This restaurant is one of our favourites and we first visited it a couple of years ago soon after it opened. We have wonderful memories associated with one particular visit.

It began as a new concept in the Trois Vallées, with an exhibition area, a sandwich bar, a traditional restaurant and a Salon Gourmand. The restaurant is beautifully fitted out and serves excellent meals if you want to splash out a bit – it's pricey for Mottaret. However, it was the Salon Gourmand that bowled us over. We decided during one especially snowy week when visibility was minimal and even Tony wasn't driven to ski from dawn until dusk, that we would choose a day to have a late lunch on the mountain, take our time over it and then return home. As this restaurant is a short ski back to our apartment along an easy path, it seemed a good choice. The leaflet we picked up said booking twenty-four hours in advance was necessary for the Salon Gourmand. This seemed over the top, but I phoned the day before.

'Bonjour Madame. Do you want the *Menu Plaisir?*'

'I don't know. What is it?'

'It's the chef's special menu. The one you have to order in advance.'

This sounded like what I wanted but I was still confused.

'What's on the menu?'

He couldn't tell me but said the chef would phone me back. This isn't going to happen, I thought. It did. Not only did the chef ring, he gave me a couple of options to choose from for the main course and told me his suggestions for the other four courses. All were fine but I'm sure they would have been changed if I'd objected. The five-course menu cost fifty euros, a lot more than a *Plat du Jour*, but this was going to be something special.

We arrived the following day in a heavy snowstorm. No lift delivers you to the door and as around twenty centimetres of fresh snow had fallen, we plodded through this to the restaurant. If I go out for a five-course meal, and that's rare, I dress carefully and make an effort to look my best. It seemed odd to be arriving hot and sticky, covered in snow, wearing ski gear. But it's a mountain restaurant. We were each given a nicely presented card with our Menu Plaisir on it. No one minded when we took our ski boots off and put them in the corner. It was a delicious meal, prepared just for us, and I'll remember the venison for a long time. The service was good but not overpowering and the chef came out to speak to us. Petit fours and Genépi, the local liqueur, were included, the *patron* bringing the Genépi. We spent two hours over the meal, having a good bottle of wine to go with it. When it was time to leave, the patron advised us not to go via the path we intended as the snow – it had snowed heavily throughout the meal – would have made it very slow. We had eaten and drunk far too much to make any serious skiing possible, especially as visibility was worsening. Getting to the path was a problem, anyway, as we couldn't see where it was. So we took the easy way out. We opted for the nearest chair lift, up to the Plattières intermediate station, and rode the cabin down. We just about managed to waddle back to the apartment. That was one of the best meals we have ever had.

With this in mind, we thought we'd look for a leaflet for this year so we could repeat the visit.

'Joe and Vic would love it. Maybe we'll all come together when they are out here.'

Joe and his wife, Vic, love their food and wine so it would be fun to introduce them to this new mountain experience. We could not, however, find any leaflets about the Salon Gourmand. I asked if the Menu Plaisir was still on offer. Sadly, it wasn't. Only one hundred people in the whole of the first season took advantage of it and as it required two extra people in the kitchen, it wasn't financially viable. It was a trial, apparently. Something tells me better marketing could have made a success of it and I am sorry we won't be able to experience it again. But I'm glad we went once.

For today, a sandwich at the sandwich bar sufficed while we reminisced about our glorious meal. It's a real suntrap, and we sat outside in deck chairs. Deck chairs in January! It doesn't happen often and we didn't stay too long there, nor did we take off anything but our gloves. We needed a few more runs to warm up and as the nearest slopes were on Mont Vallon, that's where we went.

We call this 'our' mountain as we can see it from the apartment. It needs a good covering of snow as it is basically a pile of loose rocks. It had plenty of snow today. There are two red runs here and a wide off-piste area. We got in the cabin, a poorly designed affair with a ledge running round it pretending to be a seat. It is too narrow to sit on properly and too high for a shortie like me. It's marginally better than standing up as it's a long ride to the top at a height of nearly 3000m.

We set off and turned left, skiing down a narrow path with a hairpin bend in it and a nasty drop at the corner. I used to have fears of not being able to stop at the bend and that's a sure way to make you ski badly. Some mountain re-shaping has made it much less daunting now. It's a good run down but tiring so we stopped now and then to admire the view and locate our apartment, just visible in the distance. Our legs were beginning to feel the effects of not having skied for some time, so we decided on one more trip up, then home.

There's huge pleasure in returning to our own apartment. We've rented many in the past and they are never welcoming, not the lower-end-of-the-market type we were familiar with. I think what Tony loves most about having an apartment in the Alpages is walking back to it at the end of a good day's skiing and seeing Mont Vallon shining in the sunlight behind the building, the summit just beginning to turn pink. For me, equally important is seeing our own photos and pictures on the walls, knowing that the small details of life that make it comfortable are all there. It was warm inside and we flopped onto our sofas, ignoring for once that we should have been stretching to aid the newly exercised muscles. Inertia was rushing in.

Then comes the conflict. The legs are refusing to move but the mind is saying you want a shower and the stomach is rumbling and demanding food. Nibbles are the answer. We get through far too many but they slip down so easily, especially as Tony had taken the opportunity to open a bottle of wine to go with them while he was on his feet. Just the thing after a day on the slopes. It's easy to eat and drink too much.

Our diet was something we needed to discuss. This wasn't holiday for a week or two but it wasn't normal life in

England either. What should we do about food? We had three options: eating out, buying ready-made meals or cooking properly.

'Let's buy some meat from the butcher and eat here tonight.'

I was enjoying being at home, our second home, and a restaurant would entice me another day. We bought *steak haché*, always freshly minced on request. Tony went across to the bakery and bought himself a lemon tart, a particular weakness he gives in to now and then. The *pommes dauphinois* looked good, one of the ready-made foods we do enjoy, but I decided I'd make something simple with pasta tonight, to go with the wine we'd opened.

'I'm worried about how much we'll be drinking. We're so used to drinking every day here. That's fine when we aren't here too often, but what about now?'

'We'll have to develop some self-control!'

Tony smiled.

'Maybe have some alcohol-free days.'

'Mmm. What about vins chauds? That's alcohol.'

'Oh, you're being too sensible for our first day. We'll sort it out later on.'

I only need to look at food to get fatter and practically have to starve if I need to lose weight. Tony insists the calories will all be cancelled out by the exercise. We are vastly more active than when at work, when the day's exercise consisted of walking from the desk to the loo, the printer or the coffee machine. Good job we do ski a lot as I inevitably put on weight. Tony usually loses some, curse him. Shows what a diet of French tarts can do.

We also needed some cheese. I drool at the thought of the wonderful local offerings. You can live on cheese in the Alps and I get close. There are many local cheeses of which the most famous is *Beaufort*, a hard, mature cheese with a rich, strong flavour. *Beaufort d'Alpage* is the best (and most expensive) followed closely by *Beaufort d'Eté*. Many of the local dishes involve cheese even if you don't eat it on its own. There are *raclettes*, fondues and another speciality variously called a *boîte chaude* or a *vacherin* made with the *Mont d'Or* cheese. I'm salivating as I think of it. This is a cheese available only in the winter and it comes in a small round wooden box. You place this in an oven until the cheese melts, adding white wine, and then spoon it over potatoes. You can buy this cheese in England now although when we first tasted it, it was totally new to us. We got a door-stop-sized piece of Beaufort and pretended we hadn't seen the price.

On the way back, we picked up some assorted leaflets from the Tourist Office including a new magazine to us, 'Méribel Unplugged'. When I first saw this, I assumed it was aimed at the younger visitors as 'unplugged' to me generally means what happens when I finish with the hair drier. However, it has all sorts of info and is totally in English, so despite being a Francophile, I appreciate it. While I started cooking, Tony found an interesting advertisement in it for a specialist food delivery service called 'Vallée Fare'. It was aimed at the English-speaking visitor population and offered some tempting dishes.

We phoned up the number provided and spoke to Trish. The following day's special was *ragoût* of lamb, so we ordered it.

The combination of food, drink, exercise and fresh air was beginning to tell and we went to bed early; something else that is different from our usual life in England. We were just deciding it was bedtime when Tony said, 'I've forgotten to do the lifts! Must get a master map going.'

Something we do every season is keep a tally of how many different lifts we take. There were around 160 lifts in the three valleys when we started this silly exercise and we try to do as many as possible. As a ski bum, there is every opportunity to do them all, although we draw the line at beginners' lifts. Realistically, there are only between 120 and 130 worth doing. Tony has a spreadsheet (he is an engineer, after all) and keeps a record from year to year. This sounds dreadful, but it's actually fun and has taken us to ski slopes we might otherwise have missed. There are catches to beware of – towards the end of the season, some lower lifts close so must be skied early on. One year we skied a closed slope as it looked fine at the top just to tick another lift off the list. We'll never do that again as mud skiing isn't a pleasure. To add variety, we are now trying to visit as many mountain restaurants as possible and checking those off. I don't know why I am admitting to this.

The following morning we were up later as Tony had forgotten to set the alarm. Maybe he was feeling kind. We decided we would go to Méribel, and skied down the easy Truite slope. Méribel was bustling with people.

'Let's do the Ladies' Downhill. If it's not been prepared and looks awful, we can always take the blue.'

The Ladies Downhill slope, created for the 1992 Olympic Games, is a black slope on the Les Menuires/Val Thorens side of the Méribel valley. Our confidence was returning. In good condition, it isn't a difficult black; in poor condition, it can be horrible. On one previous occasion in early April, we skied it first thing in the morning when it had thawed and refrozen. Skiing on marbles isn't my choice of conditions and it wasn't a relaxed run down. We hoped for better today. On the way up we could see parts of the piste and – great joy – it had been prepared and looked superb. There was a blue down from the top as well, a pleasant run and an escape route if we chickened out of the black. But we didn't need it. We stood at the top of the first steep section of the black and saw perfectly groomed snow, no moguls, no ice, few people. We skied from top to bottom without stopping. My heart was thumping as I concentrated. Try to keep a rhythm, get the edges in, keep the knees well bent. I know the theory but I suspect the image in my head looks better than reality.

Not far away is a small restaurant called Les Crêtes which we ear-marked for lunch. Good chips are made almost everywhere but here they are particularly tasty. This is a cosy place where orders are shouted into the adjacent kitchen and turnaround is fast. The décor is rustic with dried grasses and vegetables hanging from the roof, along with a netted ham, and although not particularly smart, it's got a great atmosphere. We once had a wonderful welcome when we arrived in a near blizzard. They were glad to see any customers as only madmen were out. The hot chocolate was lovely. Today we ordered *Soupe Flamande*. It had assorted meats in it, giving it a smoky flavour, and is different from the usual vegetable soup found all over the mountains. The waiter delivered it with panache. Wearing his hair tied in a ponytail and a brightly striped shirt, he curtseyed to me, using his apron as a skirt. A great place – we even forgive them the awful loos because they're kind.

'We should do Jerusalem while we're here.'

This is a red run down into the Belleville valley and towards St Martin. It's mentioned in a 'Ten best red runs in the French Alps' listing and is fun with lots of rollers and an interesting profile. But the best part about it is the view. We turned left out of the restaurant and skied along the ridge towards it. A curtain of snowy peaks, magnificent in the sunshine, surrounded us as we skied down. The path was easy allowing plenty of time to look around. We gathered speed on the slope itself, taking a bit of air over some of the bigger rollers.

I began to regret the Soupe Flamande as it wasn't so good the second time around. We decided it was time for a change before we did ourselves any damage and, anyway, the sun had moved. You can't see the bumps in the shade and it's colder, so we went sun-hunting on the other side of Méribel valley. An easy run across the golf course, one of the favourite beginners' areas. I thought back to the early days in Norway and how I'd appreciated the golf course for its easy gradient.

Part way down, a noise that terrifies me was getting louder, the grating sound of a fast-approaching snowboarder. I hoped he was in control. I couldn't tell which side he was coming from so I didn't know how to get out of the way. He passed on my right, closer than necessary but not unsafely. I was glad to see, literally, the back of him. We have both been knocked over by boarders in the past but I do have some sympathy for the inept boarder.

I've had a go myself using Anna's equipment when she was a dedicated boarder. We have the same size feet so swapped equipment on the mountain. I managed to get up from sitting and could turn to the left after a fashion. Going to the right was more difficult and needed to be mastered in the absence of a spiral mountain. However, the amount of face-planting puts me off and I prefer to have my legs working independently. If I were younger, I might try to acquire this skill, but I reckon it's now too late. Tony also had a go, swapping equipment with Joe. He had even more problems, finding it impossible to get up from sitting. In the end, he had to climb up Joe's leg and when he was ready, Joe leapt out of the way. Tony then went either right or left – he couldn't determine which way in advance – before falling. Neither of us feels that our future lies in boarding.

'Do you know what? We didn't stop for a vin chaud this morning!'

'Shows what happens when the conditions are really good. But I wouldn't mind one now. And a sit-down. I'm getting tired.'

We planned our route home via Côte 2000. This is a

good place to stop as it's just a short run down to get home. There are usually a few tempting desserts cunningly positioned on the bar and Tony is rarely strong enough to resist them – his ongoing love affair with French tarts. This time, along with two excellent vins chauds, he bought a *tarte aux myrtilles* laden with luscious fruit. And two spoons.

'Fruit is good for you.'

We skied home badly. The light was failing, the moguls were growing, the legs were not cooperating; it was time to stop. We were looking forward to our ragoût of lamb. It didn't disappoint.

Family Visitors

We planned to have lots of visitors. Our son, Joe, and his wife, Vic, were the first, arriving in our second week. Although much better skiers than we are, we have fun together, and if they want to go off and do silly things in the powder, we can always meet them back at the lift. Everyone in the family skis better than we do so it's easy to feel inadequate. People often ask us how good we are or, more likely, they state, 'You must be good skiers!' I never know how to respond to this as 'good' is a relative term. It all depends. I overheard a conversation between two people on a chair lift where one was explaining to the other that she was now an intermediate as she had done three weeks' skiing. So to call ourselves intermediates after over twenty-five years is a little silly. We normally go for advanced, it being lower than expert, where the kids reside. I suspect we may not even claim that in time.

We have high standards to live up to in our extended family. Many are ex-racers and Tim was in the British ski team. That's why I hesitate when folk ask if we are good skiers. Bottom line is, I suppose, we are good enough. Our main advantage is that we are about the same standard as each other. And to be a ski bum you do need to have reached a reasonable standard in order to enjoy the mountains in all their conditions and moods. Ideally, you need to be able to ski reds with confidence. Anything better than that is a bonus. We do get a kick out of skiing boldly past a group of people peering anxiously down a slope, wondering what to do. Tony has been tempted to shout, 'If Grandma and Grandpa in their sixties can do it, what are you waiting for?' But he hasn't.

Anyway, Joe and Vic feel we are good enough to ski with them – or if they don't, they are too polite to say so. Not only are they good skiers, they are good eaters and we always do well on the food and drink front with them. We decided on their first day that we would go into the Courchevel valley. We woke to sunshine and fresh snow – about twenty centimetres had fallen overnight. So it was a quick breakfast as we all wanted to be at the lift when it opened in the hope of making fresh tracks. We were amongst the first on the Pas du Lac bubbles from Mottaret to Saulire.

'Hey, nobody's coming up from Courchevel. There must be a delay in opening the lifts for some reason.'

'Perfect! Not many people up here. We may be the first down.'

We could see the tracks of a single skier ahead of us. We were not first, but close. The piste had been prepared before the new snow had fallen, so it was flat and even under the powder, and velvet on top. These are our ideal conditions. Not so deep that we couldn't cope (we're rubbish in proper powder) but deep enough to give a magical, floating feeling. The snow sparkled in the sunshine and as I followed Tony, he threw up a fine cascade of floating crystals at each turn. I couldn't imagine anyone not enjoying this. We repeated the run but the second time was poorer; the snow was already cut up and you had to seek out the unskied parts. We didn't want the disappointment of a third run.

We continued on to Courchevel 1850, posh Courchevel.

'Don't ski all the way down. Stop on the ridge above the cable car. We made a discovery last week!'

Tony was keen to show Joe and Vic a piste called *Stade de Déscente* that we'd found a few days previously. It's strange it's taken us so many years to find this but that's the joy of such a large ski area. The *Stade* is not a real *Déscente* or downhill piste but it's got some good rollers on it and is steep at the top. It had hardly been skied so we made the most of the beautiful conditions.

Just before we set off on our second run, an elderly Frenchman stopped near us. He was dressed in good quality ski gear showing signs of much use and was singing away happily in full voice. I had to say something.

'Vous êtes heureux, Monsieur?'

'Mais oui, pourquoi pas? Vous n'êtes pas malheureuse, Madame?'

'Non, pas du tout. C'est une bonne journée et la neige est delicieuse.'

'Vous êtes delicieuse aussi, Madame.'

'Vous êtes trop gentil, Monsieur.'

With that, he skied off with style, a lifetime of familiarity with the slopes giving him great ease. The French have not lost their ability to charm. Tony says I should stop chatting up old men.

When we'd had enough of the Stade, we headed for 1850 itself. I find this resort an anomaly. Parts of it, especially in the middle near the church and tourist office, are beautifully presented and the range of high-class shops is worth looking at, if not entering. Other parts are horrible.

'Vic, do you fancy spending over 100 Euros on a pair of Dior knickers! Or even more on a bra?'

I couldn't get my head around those prices. Our main purpose, however, wasn't to shop but to eat *crêpes*. One place we always visit is the Grand Marnier *crêperie*. This is a kiosk rather than a restaurant, serving crêpes on paper plates through a window. You sit on a bench or one of the low walls nearby to eat them. They are reasonably priced, served with a choice of sugar, lemon, chocolate or chestnut purée, all with loads of Grand Marnier. In fact, the large dispensing bottle of liqueur on the shelf by the hatch is a 'serve-yourself' facility. If you douse the crêpe too much, you end up drinking it off the plate! I'm afraid we did. Most un-Courchevel!

'I think there's more alcohol here than in the average vin chaud!'

Buying a vin chaud in 1850 is a bad idea, anyway. Joe warned us off doing it as he'd bought a couple the previous year in a random restaurant. They cost ten euros each, the excessive cost hardly being justified by the dreadful service.

There are more people not skiing here than anywhere else in the three valleys. An elegant lady in her twenties, wearing a soft leather coat with a thick fur collar, walked by. Her knee-length, high-heeled boots were unsuitable for snow but as she remained on the swept pavement, it wasn't a concern. An expensive bag was slung over one shoulder. Her fur hat sat slightly back on her head, showing her carefully made-up face and gold earrings to advantage. Unfortunately, the colour of her hair was too harsh to be true and that gave her away.

The Russians always get the hair dyes wrong. Courchevel 1850 is popular with them. At first, there were a few notices in Russian on some of the ski lifts, words like 'Exit', but then more appeared, and some of the glossy brochures advertising the resort had Russian versions. These relative newcomers were an important source of income for many years. Courchevel has long been a wealthy resort and there are many 'old money' people around as well. These are the ladies with the poodles, a favourite pet of the Courcheveliers. We saw a couple of beasts being carried around, their coats undoubtedly costing more than mine. If there's anything to rival crêpes in Courchevel 1850, it's people-watching.

As we'd got this far, we decided to continue on down and investigate some of the lower slopes. Going under the bridge, we turned and surveyed the backside of the town. It approaches Les Menuires for ugliness and I can't imagine paying Courchevel prices for an apartment in such a dreadful place. We left it behind and decided to head for Le Praz. This charming place had tempted us when buying our apartment as it has all the quaintness of a genuine old village. But at 1300m it's the lowest of the resorts in the Courchevel valley, and the snow is often poor at the end of the season when it thaws and then re-freezes before disappearing totally.

'We should make the most of the good conditions to ski some lower slopes. You never know how long they're going to last.'

The slope down tipped one way then the other with interesting, funny shapes. Joe led the way, the strange sideways angle of the slope causing him no problems. Tim may be the family's fastest skier but Joe takes some beating for style. I wished I could even come close. I couldn't, but even so I expect I enjoyed it as much as he did. The piste joined the romantically named *Boulevarde des Amoureux* which ended in sight of the Olympic ski jumps in the village.

We didn't eat there but went back up the mountain to the Chenus restaurant. It was busy by the time we reached it, well into the time the French eat their late lunch. I grabbed a table and the other three joined the queue. It amazes me how good the food is at most of the mountain restaurants considering everything has a long way to go to get to the kitchen.

Inevitably, Joe returned with wine. Such a bad

influence! Rabbit was today's Plat du Jour and Joe and Vic both succumbed.

'Are you really going to eat all of that?

'Just watch! I've been strong – no pudding!'

I stuck with soup and bread.

Tony was struggling to remove his boots to give his feet a rest without getting his socks wet on the floor. He surreptitiously slid the tray onto the floor to use as a foot rest.

'Are your feet hurting?'

'A bit. Usual problem with my little toes.'

The saga of Tony's boots is a long one. For many years he skied in rear entry boots, long after they had ceased to be either fashionable or recommended. They became old, much-loved friends, far too roomy to offer any support. When, as an adult male, you take size six and have extremely broad feet with a high instep, you stick with what fits. These boots met with an accident when only a few years old. After one ski holiday, they were damp and Tony put them on our boiler back home in England, not noticing he had pushed them up close to the flue, which was hot. Consequently, the front of one boot melted. Tony was distraught, but managed to reshape the boot as it cooled, mending it with bath sealant and duct tape. He was proud of the fact that he used red bath sealant and red tape to match the boots. They lasted another twelve years or so. During that time, he did buy a new pair at a Ski Show in the UK, but although he walked around in them for a couple of hours before buying, and subsequently had them stretched, he was never able to ski in them for more than an hour before they hurt. They went to a charity shop – someone got a bargain. When the famous red boots sprang a leak, it became clear that they would not last forever. A visit to Christophe became inevitable.

Christophe manages Olympic Skis in Mottaret and

over the years we have repeatedly gone to him. It was a challenge and there was hardly a boot in the place that Tony didn't try, but he succeeded. I wasn't allowed to throw the old boots away but they have finally gone. I donated them to a friend who created a flower arrangement in one of them for a Church Fête where the theme of the flower arranging was 'footwear'.

However, the no-longer-new boots aren't perfect and are an excuse for stopping at restaurants so Tony can remove them. He also carefully sits opposite me, as he was just doing, so that I can massage his toes under the table. I'm probably the only person on the mountain who has to do that. A couple of stops a day, with the appropriate treatment, and he can keep going for hours. The fashion police do, however, have to keep an eye on the trouser legs as, with all the boot removing, they have a tendency to be left at mid-calf.

We chose an easy route home via Saulire for the beautiful view, a rest and a vin chaud at Le Panoramic restaurant before the last run down into Mottaret. The sun was getting low in the sky casting a red glow over the peaks. It would be flat light on the way back as we skied out of the sunshine into the shade, so we made the most of our moments on the top.

We'd had an excellent day. Now we just needed to choose a good restaurant to finish it off.

'Any preference, Joe?'

'Let's go to Au Temps Perdu. I like it there.'

It was a favourite with us all, a cosy restaurant underground in the middle of Mottaret. We've been there many times, and Aurelie, the enchanting owner, has got to know us. On our last visit, we saw her greeting a group of French diners with the traditional two-cheek kiss, the '*bise*'. When Tony asked why we weren't greeted like that, we all got kisses too – as we did this evening. We looked at the menus that we already knew well; we'd decided what to have before we got there. We went for one of the local *Savoyarde* specialities, a *pierre chaude*. There are lots of variations on a theme amongst the local restaurants, the theme being three types of meat that you cook yourself with sauces, a green salad and chips. We knew the Temps Perdu version was a good one with 'extras': sliced vegetables to cook alongside the meat and a dish of *crozets*, which is a local pasta cooked with cream. Don't even think about the calories! Our main problem now was getting all the dishes on the table.

'I thought we were going for the pierre chaude as the healthier option rather than a fondue!'

'It is healthier. We're not cooking in oil.'

'But we're eating crozets cooked in cream!'

'It's still better than a fondue and crozets!'

Tony always has a justification for what he is going to eat. The hot stone arrived at the table and we sprinkled salt on it to prevent the meat from sticking.

'At least you can cook your beef as you like it, Dad.'

Joe was mocking Tony's taste for well-done beef, something impossible to find in France. On one occasion when he requested a well-done steak, he was told, 'No, the chef won't do it'. The customer obviously isn't always right. I've persuaded Tony to eat his beef a little rarer, so that he now asks for 'medium to well done'. The pierre chaude solves all his problems, however, and if he wants to cremate his beef, he can.

The other bonus of this restaurant is the range of home-made desserts. Tony had to make sure he'd left sufficient room, so he was careful not to eat as much meat as he might have done. The desserts are delicious and include Tony's all-time favourite, *tarte tatin*. This caramelised upside-down tart, originally made as a mistake, is a true French speciality. No two places make it exactly the same and I confess that my attempts at home fall short of the best. A couple of years ago, Tony decided that a good New Year's resolution for me (yes!) would be to make him a tarte tatin. By November of the year in question, two of my friends and our daughter had made the dessert for him – he can be very persuasive about topics close to his heart – but I hadn't got round to it. I did make one before year-end, which made me realise just how many calories they contain, but although the pastry was fine, the apples weren't right. Tony is happy for me to continue trying. I asked Aurelie what apples to use. She said that they use a Canadian apple to get the right colour and texture, so I'll now have to hunt for those.

At the end of the meal, Aurelie brought us the local liqueur, Genépi, a goodwill offering. It's potent. No one had trouble getting to sleep that night.

The following day, Joe wanted to use his new toy, a Christmas present from Vic. It was a portable GPS device, specifically designed for skiing. You wear it on your arm and it measures distance skied, height gained and speed. It can be programmed not to count travel in lifts and only measure distance in a downward direction, also giving average and maximum speeds. The competitive instinct is strong in our family and I could see that everyone would want to try this out and be the best.

'Right, we need to get out sharpish before there are too many punters around so I can have a fast run.'

This was Joe setting out the rules for the day. Made a change from Tony cracking the whip.

'I think we should head for Val Thorens. There are several slopes that might be good for a fast, straight run.'

So we headed for the Plattières lift from Mottaret.

'Mouflon's been prepared! Do we have time for a run on it?'

'Joe, you can try a fast run. There'll probably not be

many people on it.'

We could see part of the piste from the lift, in pristine condition, almost bare of people. Joe tightened his boots and adjusted the device on his sleeve. We let him go first. He set off like a rocket although I could tell he wasn't flat out. First run of the day isn't when you go fastest. We followed at our own pace and were all puffing when we gathered at a turning point a good way down. Joe was muttering to himself.

'I wonder how accurate this is. Thought I'd gone faster than that!'

He wouldn't tell us what the reading was. No doubt we'd hear when he was happy with it.

We continued on our journey to Val Thorens, arriving in the crowded central area of the resort. It's where those staying locally set off, where visitors from other valleys arrive and is a transit area when skiing between different parts of the resort. We weaved our way through the crowds, pitying the poor guys who begin their ski lives here as it's also a beginners' area.

Val Thorens is a young people's resort, but that doesn't mean it's not fun for the somewhat older. The 'young' attraction refers more to the nightlife. It's a hot spot for University ski trips – very lucrative for the resort but hell if you happen to rent an apartment in the same block at the same time. The outstanding advantage of Val Thorens is its altitude at 2300 metres.

'Let's go up the Funitel. The runs from there will give me more speed practice.'

It's a long ride up the mountain and a good rest. To Tony's amazement, I did once nod off but there's no chance of missing the top station as everyone gets off here.

We headed for Tête Ronde, a blue with lots of bends, rather like a natural downhill ski race. I haven't the nerve – or the ability – to take it straight down from the top although the temptation is there. I took the straightest line on bits of it as the conditions were so good and there were few people. The last thing you want to meet on a blind bend is a scattered group of skiers having a rest. Joe wanted to go fast, so on our second run, the three of us went ahead and stationed ourselves on the bends. We could then flag him to slow down if there were people in the way. He was lucky and on the final run out where it was wide and clear, he achieved 108 km/hr. He was happy with that; he must have been or he wouldn't have told us.

The top of the Funitel is not actually the top of the mountain. There is another lift, Glacier, which takes you to a higher, black piste, usually mogul-ridden. The usual sign was there, warning that it is for 'very good skiers only'. That's a sure way to scare! The view from the top is impressive, down to Val Thorens at 1000m below, so it's worth going up for that – as long as you can get down again. You can see the whole slope from the top of the Funitel, so in theory, you never attempt it blind. However, this proves the case that what look like small moguls from a distance, are always much larger when on them.

'We'll have to do it. It's not open often. You don't get conditions better than these.'

Joe and Vic set off for the old-fashioned two-seater lift. The slope didn't hold any fears for them. The piste hadn't been prepared since the new snow fall so I wasn't sure how good the conditions would be. I'd got bad memories of this slope. Getting down in one piece doesn't necessarily prove you are a very good skier. On one occasion, when trying to traverse across the top, the guy in front of me stopped and I didn't so we ended up in a sudden embrace which didn't impress him. Another time, I didn't see the rope at the side of the slope and skied into it. It did what it was supposed to do and stopped me, rather more forcibly and painfully than I'd have chosen. Last season, I fell on the moguls and while no damage was done, it shook me up. I felt I needed to kill the demon and ski it again.

Maybe today was the day. Maybe it was as good as it gets. I knew there was a path around the steepest part of the slope at the top, so I told myself I could take that if the prospect of the moguls from the top was too daunting. Well, they were daunting, so I headed for the path. From below, this looked easy but close up it was narrow and unprepared, a less pleasant and probably more difficult way down than the piste. I was already breathing heavily and could feel my heart thumping. Joe and Vic had set off and Tony turned towards me.

'Which way are you going? Do you want me to come with you on the path?'

I had to make my mind up. I couldn't stay there until the snow melted. The longer I hesitated, the worse it would get. I took a big breath and skied the moguls, or perhaps navigated them with care would be a better description. It's a satisfying feeling to get to the bottom having conquered the fears. I never ski moguls with panache but I do get a sense of achievement if I survive them in any sort of style.

We popped into the restaurant at the top of the Funitel for our favourite goulash soup for lunch. The atmosphere was pleasant and the berets and waistcoats the waiters wore made it feel typically French.

'Where's the loo here?'

'Ah, you're in for an experience!

Access to the loos is weird. You go through a door at the back of the restaurant, having fought your way past the self-service queue, and ascend a steep staircase with a rope handrail. You eventually arrive at two communal loos and have to wonder if the struggle was worth it. But when sufficiently desperate....

Having achieved his speed objective and skied Glacier, Joe was now hunting further moguls. For the real addict, there's a slope that is rarely flattened in Val Thorens. This is *Cascades*. I didn't want to ski it but it seemed we were doing it, anyway.

I searched for the easiest way down along the edge, cheating the mountain. The first time we skied Cascades, I froze. Tony said he would have taken a picnic if he'd known he would have to wait so long. However, we managed it more successfully this time, in spite of (or maybe because of) the pressure to perform and not let the kids down.

Tony gets neurotic if we stay too long in another valley in case we miss the last lift back. We have never missed the last lift, although I probably shouldn't have said that. It was getting towards three o'clock and the weather was changing. We'd lost the sun and could see clouds swirling around.

'This might be the fog they promised us. Let's head back.'

By the time we got back into our valley, the fog had come in and visibility was down to a few metres, a real white-out. The change was rapid. I don't like skiing in fog. It's easy to get disorientated and even nauseous.

'We need to stay within sight of each other and of the piste markers. We'll ski along the edge of the piste. I'll go first'.

Tony led us out in single file and we progressed well but then lost the markers. We all stopped together and peered into the greyness. There was no one else around. Sensible folk had returned earlier. We spread out, still within sight of each other to see if we could spot a marker. Vic saw one so we followed her and gathered at the wooden stick marking the edge of the piste.

'Right, I think I know where we are now. If we ski to the left of this, we'll follow a piste that takes us to the middle of Mottaret.'

Tony is a good guide and I never argue with him. My sense of direction was discarded with the placenta. Joe, however, disagreed.

'You'll be off-piste if you go to the left. We need to go to the right of this marker.'

The two men looked at each other, both convinced they knew what to do.

'Who skis here the most?'

'Okay, you win.'

We agreed to follow Tony, fortunately not too closely as within seconds he had disappeared into a hole full of soft snow. He was unhurt although it took him a considerable time to fight his way out. The sight of first a ski, then a pole, then an arm or a leg appearing, and then disappearing, caused us much amusement. Joe refrained from the almost inevitable, 'I told you so' and went to help. Vic and I were in a hopeless mess with laughing so much and in great need of a loo as a consequence. A learning point is that piste markers on the left of the slope when heading down are a single colour whereas those on the right have a coloured band at the top. Or is it the other way round....?

Strangely, we continue to trust Tony's sense of direction. And it wasn't the last time he led us astray. There was the memorable time, a few years later, when he skied off the edge of a piste in the mist and had to be rescued by Anna. But I digress.

Joe and Vic's last evening arrived and they decided we should go out for a drink.

The choice of where to drink is huge but as we mostly drink *chez nous*, we didn't have a list of places to suggest. But the children's generation knows about these things. Our kids take us in hand.

We went to Scotts Bar first, right in the middle of Méribel. Everyone was speaking English. There were

Scottish, Welsh and Canadian accents but not a French voice anywhere. I went to the bar and tried to order some drinks in French. That was a silly idea. All the staff were Australian. We now call it our regular bar as we've been there at least three times. That's three times in about seven years. I noticed an advertisement there for a talk one evening called 'Méribel – so British'. I decided not to go.

Another particularly English bar, frequented by *seasonaires* – ski instructors and the like – is Barometer. So we ambled over there a little later. While lively and fun, I prefer a more French place. So my needs were met and we went to La Poste, next to the post office. It had subtle lighting, good décor and was swish. It offered a wide range of cocktails and wasn't cheap – but that's drinking in posh bars for you! That was enough for me. I wasn't interested in continuing my drinking career in a club. A whole book could be written about drinking in nightclubs in the ski resorts. I am not qualified to write it.

Specially Prepared...

Time between visitors is also fun, time for ourselves, reading, crosswords, watching a film or two. It's good to ski with friends but it's good to ski with just the two of us. After Joe and Vic left, we decided we'd have a long day out. We went to bed thinking we'd wake early, unprompted by the alarm clock and we could then decide where to go. Snow was forecast to fall overnight with sunshine to follow, so conditions sounded perfect. When I woke, I could see it was light although the curtains were drawn so I peered at my watch to see how late it was. Just half past seven, not late at all. I reached out and lifted a corner of the curtain. Snow was falling heavily, swirling around in the gusting wind that had blown a few flakes through the open window. A snowplough was already at work, clearing the road and part of the car park, bleeping as it reversed. I closed the window and pulled the duvet over me, the short time out of bed already chilling me. I'd disturbed Tony so he rolled towards me, our bodies wrapping around each other, his early morning warmth familiar and comforting. There was no rush to get up. Neither of us fancied skiing in a blizzard. The luxury of a lie-in, no pressure to do anything, was overwhelming. The jigsaw of our forty years of marriage was still fully interlocking. There are not many activities that will keep Tony away from the slopes but I can think of one.

We got up sometime later, showered and had a relaxed breakfast. The weather forecast had not been entirely wrong, just out with its timing as the snow had stopped and the day was improving. Patches of blue were appearing, oddly shaped fish swimming across the clouds. By the time we got out on the slopes, the new snow was cut up but it was still good skiing. We went to Courchevel, heading towards the 1650 area, and joined the short queue for the rapid six-man chair, heading for the *Piste du Jour*, Chapelet. Tony suddenly pulled up and I skied across to see why. He was pointing at the sky. The sun had broken through a patch of cloud and the rosy light was exquisite, almost spooky.

Just near the lift is a smart restaurant, La Casserole. The menu looks good but we only go in for drinks on account of the prices. The tables were laid for lunch but a waitress found us a bare one near the door to the kitchen. It felt like sitting in the cheap seats at the theatre but it was warm and had the advantage of being near the display of tarts. Tony was seduced. He bought a large slice of raspberry and myrtille, with two spoons. There was a delicious layer of frangipane between the pastry and the fruit. I don't know what he paid for it; it's better not to know. I took in again the lovely décor of the place, lots of embroideries on the walls, traditional samplers as well as cows and other animals, and imaginative and interesting decorations around the lights. I hesitate to call them Christmas decorations in January but that's really what they are. I used my previous knowledge of the place to use the nice loos by the posh restaurant rather than the below-standard ones adjacent to the self-service area. I popped along when the waiters weren't watching as they don't approve of cross-looing.

I had a glance at another restaurant, Bel Air, not far away as we skied by. I was looking for one of its characters, a remarkable, leather-faced lady who graces the terrace for long periods, ensuring that the damage she is doing to her skin is beyond the help of any moisturiser. But January was too early and too cold for her.

We headed back out of the valley via Col de la Loze. The ancient two-man chair is possibly the slowest in the Three Valleys. It is the type that thumps you on the back of the legs when you try to get on it. The lift attendant rarely moves from the small hut to help; kindlier ones catch the chair for you. Tony took the biggest thump to save me. It was getting colder and we sat close together to hide from the wind. A long, slow lift gives you a good rest but this one wasn't restful.

Folk were milling around as we got off, debating the best way back. The snow had blown off most of the surface which was hard-packed and shiny. It was difficult to see what was ice and what was rock. We slithered towards the pistes, deciding against the busy blue boulevard and the dodgy black. We set off down the oddly named Pic Noir, a winding red. I groaned out loud as my ski grated against a rock I'd not spotted. It's almost as painful as grazing a knee when you feel a rock tear into the smooth ski base. I should have seen it, a sign my attention was wavering. We skied across the golf course to the rapid Altiport chair, the first leg on our way back to Mottaret. I was wedged in alongside a large lady. Her phone rang and she answered it.

'*Da.*'

We had Russians beside us. The stressed, sombre tone of the Russian language made her conversation sound as if she was organising the next summit of world leaders. She wasn't an elegant Russian. Something happens between the ages of thirty and fifty, hiding slim, fashion-conscious women inside robust, large-lipped, course-featured *babuschkas*. The only thing they have in common is the badly dyed hair. Most of my paltry Russian had long been forgotten so I turned my attention to the heavily laden spruce trees either side of the lift. The new snow was bending the branches in arcs and every so often, the weight would become too much and the snow would slide off. The bare branch of a tree we were passing suddenly sprang upwards spraying snow around, the cones at its tip pointing podgy fingers at us.

We were going out to eat that night at Le Brizolée, a popular place just a short walk from the apartment. It was packed when we arrived. I peeled off my warm layers as we sat down. A profusion of heaters for the various Savoyarde specialities had raised the temperature to tropical levels. We chose a *raclette* so I could indulge my passion for cheese. The large chunk of cheese was brought on its heated stand. We each had little wooden shovels to scrape the melted cheese onto our potatoes and charcuterie.

'We're not going to be able to eat all this cheese.'

'We never do, but I doubt anyone does. I bet they'd be surprised if we did.'

We made an admirable effort and consumed more cheese than we normally do in a week in England. After coffee, we wrapped ourselves up and walked home. I tapped in the code on the front door to the apartment building and pushed. It didn't open.

'Do it more slowly. It didn't register properly.'

I tried again but with no luck.

'I think you overcompensated and did it too slowly that time. Let me do it.'

Tony was sure it was operator error as we'd never had a problem before. But he had no success either. Earlier in the day, the door had not been closing properly and we concluded a security-minded inhabitant had locked the door on the inside. This meant it could only be opened with a key. Our keys remained inside the apartment. The Syndic provides a good service and holds a set of spare keys but not twenty-four hours a day. It was close to eleven o'clock. There weren't many people in the building although we had spoken to our neighbours earlier that week.

'Go round the back and see if their light is on. If it is, knock on the window and explain. They'll let us in.'

Tony plodded through thigh-deep snow to the back of the building. This was one occasion our neighbours had chosen to have an early night. There were two lights visible on the second floor but we didn't think they would hear us shouting and sounding the horn was anti-social at that time of night. The temperature was minus five degrees and snow was falling. By chance, Tony had the car keys in his pocket so we sat in the car with the engine running to think and keep warm.

'The last bus will be up from Méribel soon. There'll possibly be someone from our building on it.'

That evening, there was no last bus.

'I saw someone with a dog coming out of the building yesterday. If he's still here, the dog might need a last pee.'

It's not often that the only hope of a proper night's rest depends on a dog needing to relieve itself. Shortly before midnight, we decided a night in the car was inevitable. Tony had just disappeared to the corner of the car park to have a pee himself, and I was hoping I would not need to, when the longed-for dog and owner appeared. I am now an ardent dog-lover. It was a wonderful night's sleep.

Eyeore on the Slopes

I love Eyeore, Winnie the Pooh's gloomy donkey friend. I have an Eyeore keyring hanging on a hook in the apartment. I wish he'd stay there. But sometimes he has an urge to join us on the slopes. He did the following day. We set off in sunshine to ski in the Menuires valley.

'I hadn't realised how cold it was.'

'Nor me. You'd think we'd get it right by now. I don't think I've got enough layers on.'

The worst of it was that we had several chair lifts to ride. On Côte Brune, which we call the fridge, I tried sitting on one hand to warm it up. It helped so I tried to sit on both hands. That was dodgy as I risked dropping the poles wedged between my knees.

'Do you think we should go in for a vin chaud at the top to warm up?'

Tony was as cold as I was but I didn't think we could possibly start the day like that.

'Let's just have a vigorous ski and warm ourselves up that way.'

I felt stiff and awkward with no flexibility. There was no excuse as the snow was great. Tony got further away from me as his skis moved beautifully over the well-prepared piste. I skied up to him when he stopped.

'You're skiing well. I feel like a pregnant cow. Nothing is working. I don't seem to have any bounce and

I'm sliding around. I thought our standards were similar but they're not anymore.'

'You need warming up. My skis are running well, that's all.'

I warmed up a bit but was still muttering when we got the chair back up. Fortunately, this one was in the sun and had a cover on it. Still cold, we gave in and went into Alpage, an attractive chalet with its ribbon-tied twigs and painted enamel coffee pots.

'Last time we had a vin chaud here, it was so sweet I couldn't finish it. And there was no fruit. The only drink to beat me.'

I was not in a good mood today.

'Well, maybe it'll be better today. You can warm your hands on it, anyway. I didn't realise that Eeyore was with us.'

The vin chaud was sweeter than the last time.

From the restaurant we could see a piste often used for races and race training as it lends itself well to giant slalom turns with its bends and swoops. It was in perfect condition so we headed for it. We skied from top to bottom twice. There was no one on it but us, not even Eeyore. There was a downside – the drag lift had a particularly strong spring on it and not only did it fire us off, it left me most uncomfortable for several hours, a 'blue bottom' ride. Brought back memories of early skiing in Norway.

But the improvement in my skiing was temporary and when we got home, Tony looked at me seriously and said, 'I think we'll visit Christophe tomorrow and get you some new skis.'

We tend to forget how long we keep equipment for. Tony loved his previous skis and hadn't planned on replacing them until Tim borrowed them one day, his own having been stolen. Tony was interested to hear what Tim thought of them. He was expecting a comment along the lines of, 'Not bad – but not stiff enough for me,' or 'Okay – about right for you.'

So it came as a shock when Tim's single comment was, 'Crap'. Apparently, they were worn out. Suddenly the much-loved skis were less loved, didn't turn as well and had no edges. It was back to Christophe and after trying out a few pairs, Tony bought new ones. It certainly speeded up his skiing and with a stiffer pair, he felt far more stable and his overall performance improved. We should have realised that the consequence of Tony's improvement would be my dissatisfaction. It was just a matter of when it would happen.

We were at the shop early next morning, explaining the situation. Christophe wanted to know what I was looking for. That was a good question as I didn't know.

'I just want to try something better than I've got.'

I was skiing on Salomon, so I decided to try the latest version of that model. I set off with great expectations but was disappointed. There was no magic. The skis felt much like the ones I had already but with better glide and sharper edges. I used them for a day and returned them to Christophe.

'What else do you have?'

'As you're short, there's not much choice. But these are different. They're stiffer, more advanced – you might like to try.'

He offered me a pair of Atomic M2tron skis. These were 152cm, the shortest I'd ever skied on and the heaviest I'd ever lifted. Just shouldering them was a major effort so I wasn't greatly optimistic. I had the feeling all skis would feel the same and the problem was me. Good old Eeyore was alive and well!

The next morning we set off and disaster struck immediately. Tony was skiing behind me to watch how I was doing. These skis were certainly different; I couldn't ski on them.

'I can't turn. I think they're just too stiff for me. They're dreadful. If I can't ski on this slope, I'll never manage anything more difficult!'

We were heading down into Courchevel on Creux, a wide slope in good condition and almost empty. Tony was working out the quickest route back to Christophe's shop to put me out of my misery when he had an idea.

'Maybe they've been sharpened too far along their length for you. Remember you had a problem with turning last time your own skis were sharpened.'

He produced some emery paper from his rucksack, always the well-prepared man, and rubbed the edges towards the tips and tails. A couple of minutes later, the world began to change. Not only could I now turn, the skis were immensely stable and my confidence grew by the minute.

'I can't believe this. These are great! I feel so safe on them.'

There is nothing like confidence to improve performance. I was not only skiing far better than I'd done in ages but I was floating above the ground, I felt so good. By the end of the day, I'd decided I would buy a pair.

'They've transformed your skiing. You're a different skier from yesterday. Unbelievable in such a short time.'

I returned to Christophe and ordered the new skis. Buying them was one good decision.

Our equipment sorted, the time was right to take out Joe's GPS device and see how far we travelled in a normal day.

'This isn't a competition, you know. I still want to be able to have lunch and drink stops. Just covering a huge distance on our skis doesn't make it more enjoyable.'

'I know. It's just fun to find out what distance we cover. I really have no idea. I'm not intending it to be an obsession. The kids would always beat us, anyway.'

He lied, he lied! It wasn't about the kids; what he wanted to do was prove he was faster than me!

We set off for Courchevel, deciding to go to its highest point at 2705m.

The guy who mans the lift here wins our prize for best-kept lift station. He manicures his snow walls at the top, has welcome signs in the snow and has put up signposts pointing out the view of Mont Blanc. As we arrived, he was moving snow around, making sure the area was neat and tidy. His little hut was immaculate, even boasting curtains, and his Christmas decorations still looked good, as did his Christmas tree. A lonely life but he obviously enjoys it. We were sad when he retired – but he warranted an article in the local newspaper.

We skied on down to Courchevel, stopping to look back at our tracks. Had we actually managed to carve? Could we see beautiful parallel grooves? Well, maybe, but there were too many tracks to be sure. This wide-open area of Courchevel was fun, plenty of space so it rarely felt crowded. Today it was deserted, hardly anyone in sight. I was skiing behind Tony when I suddenly realised that we were heading for the same patch of snow.

'We're getting far too close!'

I yelled out but it was too late. As I turned left, Tony turned right. We hit head-on. Four skis released and scattered around the slope. I lost a pole and slid a few metres down the slope, shipping a load of snow under my jacket and all over my sunglasses. I stopped, relieved to find I was intact, no damage to anything. I could see Tony about twenty metres below me. He had easily won the sliding-down-the-snow race. I gathered my equipment, cleaned my glasses and shook out what snow I could. Finding a flattish place to re-set my bindings and put my skis back on was a problem but I eventually joined Tony, also unhurt.

'How can we hit each other on a wide, empty slope?'

'Must be our magnetic attraction. Sorry, it was my fault. I shouldn't have skied so closely behind you, but I was going well, I didn't notice I was catching you up. Must be the new skis.'

'Well, we've survived. You stay on the right and I'll stay on the left. We might not be as lucky next time.'

We headed down towards Courchevel 1850, along the easy wide slope we call 'Swank Alley'. The beautiful chalets along one side undoubtedly cost several times that of our house in England. Massive wood, little bell towers, elegant designs; I would just love to see inside one but no one I know is ever likely to afford such a place. Mostly owned by Russians, we believe.

For lunch, we stopped at the popular Bouc Blanc above La Tania. We'd tried this restaurant once before but it had been so crowded and the service so slow that we moved on. It was quite late by the time we got there so hoped for better luck. No one seemed interested in showing us to a table and all were covered with the debris of earlier diners. We sat down at one and tried to catch a waitress's eye. Within a few minutes, a harassed young girl cleared the table, dumping the dirty plates and glasses on another, equally messy table alongside. She rushed off without taking our order. I could see Tony fidgeting, wondering whether to put his jacket back on and leave. Our waitress had disappeared so I waved at another.

'J'arrive!'

Eventually, she did and we ordered soup. Mine arrived quickly. I'd almost finished and there was still no sign of Tony's. Again, I called over the waitress, who had clearly forgotten he hadn't been served. Ultimately we both enjoyed the soup and the price was reasonable. But there was no welcome from any of the staff, too rushed to be friendly. The stuffed head of a goat – the bouc blanc – on the wall gave us the closest we got to a smile. (However, we gave them another chance and were third time lucky. It's now one of our favourite places!)

We began to wend our way back to our valley, taking the Dou des Lanches chair lift.

'We ought to ski the piste here so we can tell Chris we've gone past his tree.'

A few years before we'd skied this black slope with Anne-Berit and Chris, our friends from Norway. Chris had lost control and had managed to stop about a metre short of a large tree beside the piste. We'd all watched in horror, expecting the worst. Anne-Berit was mentally searching for the will. Fortunately, it wasn't needed but it was an event that lodged itself in all our memories. Today, we both had problems holding an edge, the steepness and polish challenging us. A snowboarder was also having trouble and had positioned herself in the middle of the piste for a rest. As I turned above her, I skidded and narrowly missed her fingers. Well, there was a gap of a few centimetres. She probably still remembers the shock I gave her and I remember her yell.

Tony had been inspecting the GPS from time to time but hadn't told me how we were doing. Back in the apartment, he announced we had skied a marathon and descended an Everest.

'That's impressive!'

'Actually it sounds more impressive than it really is. I bet if the kids tried they'd do far more.'

'I thought we said this wasn't a competition?'

Tony had also managed a maximum speed of 70km/hr, not bad for a Grandpa.

However, although we believed these numbers, my faith in the device wavered when Tony produced 113km/hr a day later. As he wasn't trying and wasn't even going straight, it seemed unlikely to be true. However, he got immense satisfaction from it, told everyone and recorded it in our Visitors' book.

Mind the Mundane

There are disadvantages to being out in the apartment for a long period. One is getting the laundry done. I discovered a launderette in Méribel, a short drive away. I hadn't used a launderette since early in our marriage and it wasn't an experience I was relishing. Nevertheless, it had to be done, so we set off with two large sacks of washing. We went in the evening, of course, so as not to lose good skiing time, but found that all the chalet/gap year girls and guys did the same. There were no available machines. The place was packed, everyone younger than us by at least thirty-five years. Girls were struggling with folding machine-loads of sheets, the corners dragging on the damp, dirty floor. There was a quirky guy in the corner, his fierce tattoos at odds with his skinny arms, forlornly reading a discarded leaflet as his mixed wash shared a common colour and everything ended up in shades of grey. I felt we were an anomaly.

We drove back up the mountain and had a second go an hour later. I had just loaded a machine when one of our young washing colleagues pointed out that the establishment closed in ten minutes' time.

'Let's just risk it. They can't lock us in.'

'They can make us leave our washing here. I don't want to have to get it tomorrow.'

We unloaded the machine and returned home. To say I was less than pleased would not do justice to the situation. Okay, I'm spoiled but it would have been bad enough if it had all gone smoothly. We did manage to get the washing done later in the week. We beat the rush by about thirty seconds so I suppose I should be glad. However, as if to compensate, we found our car wheels spinning when we tried to pull out of the sloping parking place. Luckily we had a shovel with us and a combination of digging and pushing got us on our way. I was now sweating and sticky from the exertions as well as generally fed up. My gloves felt like slimy fish with all the water they had soaked up. I had dirt on my jeans from brushing against the filthy car. The cuffs of my jacket showed the grime of a miner. I felt like jumping into a washing machine myself. I may have to investigate the market opportunity of opening another launderette.

The apartment looked beautiful with drying laundry festooned around it. The time in the spin dryer had hardly removed any moisture, so we put up with the decorations for a couple of days, moving them from place to place as they got in the way.

'I hate this, I hate it! I hate it!'

In desperation, Tony has said that he will take the washing to the laundrette on his own in future in order to maintain household calm. I'll have to learn to love the drying scenario.

Another service I'd not previously needed was that of a hairdresser. I really couldn't last all season without looking like a mobile hedge. So I wandered into the local Mottaret beauty salon one Friday afternoon after skiing, to see if Hélène could fit me in. It was a remarkable experience. She talks rapid French the whole time, to anyone and everyone, and naturally expects to be understood. I wondered how much attention my hair would get as she keeps an eye on everything going on. You certainly can't get out in a hurry. No question of what I wanted done; she simply ran her hands through my hair.

'I give you a good cut.'

Her style of cutting seemed random, unlike my hairdresser back home. But it worked. It was superb.

While having my hair shampooed, the beauty therapist came and looked at my skin. Inevitably, after the exposure that comes with skiing, even with the use of high factor sun cream, my skin needed some attention and she suggested a facial. I said I would think about it. I never go in for such extravagances. But what the hell! A couple of days later, I was back to book an appointment for the works.

'Come here. I'll comb your hair up for you.'

Hélène called me across. What a treat! No charge but part of the service. A lovely touch. I had the facial and yet again, Hélène offered to tidy my hair. She looks after her customers.

'Next time, you'll have to visit me in Brides les Bains at my salon there.'

'It's much more convenient here.'

'For you, yes, but the salon in Brides is my own; I rent up here and will not be continuing.' Her mother would be managing the Mottaret salon. At a later date, *Maman* cut my hair, also promising 'a good cut', talking frantic French all the time, moaning about her water bill – *'Oh, là-là!'* – claiming at sixty-eight she was too old and fat to ski, and being most definitely the boss towards the more junior hairdressers. She was just like her daughter, but larger and noisier.

On one occasion, all the lights went out. Much panic and many more cries of *'Oh, là-là!'* Assistants rushed to other shops to see if the problem was widespread and Maman had an agitated phone conversation with, it turned out, an answering machine. When the lights came back on, I asked if it had ever happened before.

'Yes, all the time!'

95

I'd not have guessed.

She called me her *petite anglaise* and I found her, with all her eccentric ways, a delightful and friendly lady.

Friends

Dave and Barbara, friends from England, were arriving the following day and we'd arranged to meet them in Moûtiers. We hadn't used the car since we arrived and it was covered in snow so we set about it with the shovel. It wasn't too bad a job, the snow still being light and the shovel large. A shovel is a rare possession, it seems; we have seen people digging with skid pans, skis, even large spoons. A rent-a-shovel service is probably a business opportunity waiting to be exploited. We were all set to go, allowing plenty of time so that we could visit the large supermarket in Moûtiers, but the car wouldn't move. The wheels were spinning on the ice beneath them. Folk are kind and a group of young men helped us on our way with a few hefty pushes.

The roads were clear but we were worried about the forecast which promised snow during the evening. We had chains with us, a legal requirement in the Alps. They were new ones, easier to put on than our old, problematic set. We stocked up in the supermarket, the range of goods being excellent and the prices more reasonable than up the mountain. There was a vast choice of French wine, shelf after shelf offering wines of all prices. The section for the rest of the world was about a metre wide. Good job we wanted to buy local!

It had just begun to snow when our friends arrived. Snow isn't always good news. Not when you need to drive up the winding roads to Mottaret. Conditions deteriorated as we moved up the mountain. The hope of making it without chains disappeared and about twenty minutes from our apartment we had to stop. Tony and Dave got out the chains while Barbara and I stayed in the car. They were both engineers, after all, so we left them to it. We could hear their conversation.

'Just pass the chains over the top of the tyre and I'll grab the hook. I should be able to link it then.'

'I can't get my hand far enough under the wheel arch.'

'Let's swap positions and I'll have a go.'

'I thought these were meant to be the easy-to-put-on chains.'

'That's what it says on the box.'

There was a lot of muttering and cursing then they both got back into the car to warm up. Whenever you need chains, it's dark, cold, snowing and the car is filthy. Tony had forgotten his head torch and his old jacket; he ruined his decent gloves. Dave wasn't expecting to be chain-man's assistant. They gave up. Barbara and I said nothing. We made it as far as we could, parked the car and got a taxi. Tony rescued the car in better conditions the following day.

Question: How many engineers does it take to put chains on a car?

Answer: More than two.

Moral: Read the instructions properly, preferably when it's not dark, cold or snowing.

We were rather more successful on skis than we'd been on wheels. Dave and Barbara first skied with us when we lived in Norway. They were beginners when they visited us there with their two children and the plan was that all the kids would ski together, Tony would ski with Dave and I would ski with Barbara. That way, everyone would learn. Then I broke my leg a couple of weeks before they arrived so rather than skiing I was hobbling around on crutches. I hold myself responsible for Barbara not learning to ski; she spent more time chatting to me than practising with the others. The net result was that we never thought we'd be able to ski together. Then around ten years ago, Barbara said they would join us on our next ski holiday. We were delighted.

'What's the plan? Do you want to join a group class or would you rather have a private lesson or two?'

'I don't know. I'll wait until we get there and then decide.'

'If you like, you could come out with us on an easy slope, just to get the feel.'

'We'll see. Let me think about it.'

So nothing more was decided and we arrived at the apartment. We pestered Barbara about her decision, but she said she'd tell us on the first morning, when she'd finally made her mind up.

We sat down to breakfast, eager to find out what Barbara's plans were. I was so looking forward to being out on the mountain together.

'I'm staying here. I've decided I don't want to ski after all.'

We all looked at each other in the long pause that followed.

'But that's awful! What'll you do? It'll be so boring!'

'No, it won't. I've thought it all through. I've plenty to read. I'll go for walks, and you know I like people-watching. Don't worry about me.'

There was no persuading her otherwise. I didn't like leaving her behind, but the call of the snow was great. Barbara is dear to me but a skiing holiday on foot was not amongst my plans. So that was the pattern for that year and for future ski holidays. I always feel guilty leaving her in the apartment but she insists I shouldn't.

The three of us set off early the next morning, determined to cram as much into our week together as possible. Dave only skis once a year, so we try to cover as much of the Three Valleys with him as possible. I think we are over-generous, Dave might say sadistic, in the number of hours skiing we give him. The guy does brilliantly in the face of the challenges we throw at him and still comes back for more.

'Day one, so no blacks,' Tony said. Dave agreed.

We decided on an early morning Mouflon. It looked inviting.

'We're not first here; people have come up from Les Menuires and beaten us.'

'Well, I did my best but I can't make an old lift go fast.'

'Hey, Dave, do you remember going the wrong way here?'

'I certainly do! You go first.'

Dave normally follows us, but on one occasion in this spot had set off first. We'd just had a last vin chaud at the top of the mountain and were preparing to ski back into Mottaret. From the restaurant, you can also ski into the Menuires valley, and that's what Dave did. He couldn't hear our shouts as he disappeared in the wrong direction. Hindsight told us Tony should have chased him, but we assumed he would realise his error and get the lift back up immediately so we just waited. This was before mobile phones. He eventually stopped and realised we weren't with him. The nearest lift was closed so he skied on and found another lift, about to close. In desperate French, he got his message across and fortunately the lift guy took pity on him. By this time, we had given up and were back at the apartment, explaining to Barbara we had lost her husband. It takes a couple of hours to drive from Mottaret to Les

Menuires, and we were about to dig the car out when an exhausted Dave turned up. Having got back up from the Menuires valley and not knowing which way to go other than down towards Mottaret, he ended up on Bartavelle, a black in poor condition. He survived – and it makes a good story. The term 'Doing a Dave' has gone into our skiing vocabulary. Note: if you must get stuck in the wrong valley, choose Courchevel as the taxi ride back costs less than from Les Menuires. And definitely don't get caught in the fourth valley!

After Mouflon, we thought Mont Vallon would be a good bet.

'You need some speed or you'll have to plod the last part so try to get a good schuss near the bottom of the slope.'

Tony went first, followed his own advice and navigated his way through the crowd of people milling around the lift queue. I spotted a clear route and reckoned my speed would get me to the right place. There was a gap of a couple of metres I was aiming for when a guy in a yellow jacket skied into it. I was going far too fast and although I tried to brake, it was too late. I hit the yellow jacket, bounced off and splatted on the snow, losing both skis.

'Pardon, Monsieur, pardon, desolée.'

It was totally my fault and I felt dreadful. The guy I hit said nothing. My impact had simply moved him a metre or so. He just looked at me with no emotion and looked away. Maybe he wasn't French and hadn't understood my apology. I was expecting a tirade about irresponsible skiing, a tirade I deserved, but nothing. I picked myself up, retrieved my skis and joined Tony and Dave, a little shaken. I haven't done that again. If anyone hits me now, I try to show some sympathy.

The following day, Tony wasn't feeling well and

stayed in bed (an unusual occurrence as little keeps Tony off the slopes), so I acted as Dave's guide. Not sure if he realised the risk he was taking! Anna later asked me if we spent the entire day going up and down Mouflon. We didn't – we skied widely over the Méribel valley. To say I planned our route would be stretching the truth but we didn't get lost. I discovered many interlinking slopes and wasn't always sure where we would end up. However, when we got there I was able to plan the next bit. On our way back to the apartment, we skied past the top of *Grand Rosière*. This is a black slope we don't often ski and I'd noticed a sign on the way out saying it had been specially prepared. I asked Dave if he was up for it. He was. It was in good condition and we were the only two on it. I set off at a reasonable pace and Dave came past me like a rocket. He stopped at the bottom and looked back to see me way behind. I don't know which of us he frightened most. And whether or not he was in control remains an open question. That guy's got bottle!

Tony never gives up where getting Barbara to ski is concerned. He thought we might be able to get her on Joe's blades as they are less daunting than full-length skis. These are mini, fun skis about 90cm long, that you use without poles. Dave was keeping out of this discussion, wise man, and I was ambivalent, not wanting to upset Barbara. Tony can't understand anyone not wanting to ski and he set about the conversion with missionary zeal. The first task was to find boots to fit her. Mine were too small but Tony thought his would do.

'If I try on a boot, what will you do in return? It has to be something unpleasant.'

'I'll eat some blue cheese.'

With much face-pulling and making of disgusting noises, Tony ate a minute piece of blue cheese. Barbara found that the boot fitted. Shades of Cinderella here although Tony was hardly the prince. The plan was for

Barbara to try skiing on the blades the following evening, after the lifts had closed. The slope by the beginners' rope tow would be adequate as our aims were modest. Barbara spent the day trying to think up some horrible task for Tony to do in return for her efforts but failed.

'I don't have to walk to the slope in the ski boots, do I?

'That was the plan.'

'They're not that comfortable. I'm not doing that.'

Tony wasn't easily defeated and said he would carry the boots. I lent her a ski jacket as she didn't have ski clothing. She looked worried as we set off. Dave was silent. Tony grinned. I gave her a hug.

Barbara has natural balance – she used to ice-skate. With her hands on her knees to get her weight in the right position, she skied about ten metres, even managing a snowplough stop. We all cheered and I don't think it's a total overstatement to say that Barbara almost enjoyed it. We have the video to prove she did it. It was certainly not as difficult as she expected and there was a smile on her face. So Tony achieved his aim but I doubt this is the beginning of a ski career for Barbara. She doesn't like speed or heights and isn't keen on ski lifts. Not the best pre-requisites for skiing. But she was a good sport. And she still has to get her revenge on Tony; she's working on it.

Tony, by way of compensation, decided the men should cook the following evening. He instituted a men's cooking night a few years ago and various male visitors have been co-opted to help out, whether they wanted to or not. No one has hit him yet. The guys did cheat a bit this time. We had a combined pierre chaude and raclette, where everyone cooks their own food at the table. However, they did go and buy the ingredients, lay the table, cook the potatoes, put various sauces and salad in bowls and, more importantly, pour generous glasses of wine and provide nibbles for Barbara and me.

The first part of our season was all but over. We just had to write in our guest book. When we first bought the apartment, Anna gave us a Visitors' book, inscribed with *Chez Fawke* at the front. We ask everyone who stays to write in it, whether they are with us or on their own. And without exception, everyone has. We also make entries. It includes hints and tips on restaurants, weather reports, drawings, a complete eight-verse poem and best of all, stories. It's great to read back through it and relive the moments. We can chart the skiing progress of the Bailey family, friends who always use the apartment at English half-term, across eight years now. The children's handwriting has improved no end, as has their skiing, and they are the main contributors to the illustrations. Maybe reading the book will be the ultimate skiing substitute when we are no longer able to do anything else. Dave noticed an earlier comment he'd made: *Another wonderful week although my body feels as though it has been through the wringer. The time between vin chauds seems to get longer.* Funny how nothing changes.

Barbara spotted her contribution: *Had a trip up Plattières to join the skiers for lunch and didn't feel too travel sick after riding the bubble lift.*

'That must have been a brave day!'

None of us was keen to take Tim's advice: *If there are no obvious tracks through a mogul field, go straight!*

Our own entries were the most numerous and it was good to re-live and laugh at some of the memories.

Had some good French practice sorting out the key to the ski room locker which decided not to work (hence no access to our skis – amazing what necessity can achieve!)

If anyone else is as mad as we are and insists on skiing in the rain, two hours is long enough to get completely wet! (Note: some sense has come with retirement.)

Our powder skiing has improved to bad.

We'd planned to return home together. We can just about squash all of us and our belongings into our car. No problems with chains this time as the weather was good. February is a busy month for ski resorts. Half-term in France is scattered through the month and English half-term brings floods of Brits to the Three Valleys. No sensible retiree would ski then and we don't. We planned to return to England for three to four weeks, resuming our bumming life at the end of the month. We were indulging our fondness for wine again on the way home.

Tony had booked an overnight stop in Nuits St Georges, keen to introduce our friends to one of the good wine areas. We arrived at the Gentilhommière. This was a sixteenth century hunting lodge rather than a true château. Tony had a long face when we were shown our rooms. They were 'standard' as booked, nicely furnished and modern, but were an addition to the main building and didn't have the old-fashioned charm we'd come to expect on our travels.

'Not a good choice. Especially as we've got Dave and Barbara with us.'

'We're getting spoiled, but I know what you mean.'

The guidebook did indicate a *'restaurant gastronomique'* and that raised our spirits. It was in the main building, which was beautiful, and we chose one of the fixed menus. It had to be a Burgundy wine and we were going to choose a Nuits St Georges as the most appropriate. However, at a price of 70€ minimum, we decided a good white Burgundy would do. And it did excellently. The waiter offered us English and French menus which helped with some of the stranger culinary terms. We all chose 'chest of pork' as our main course, intrigued as to what it might be. It turned out to be fatty belly pork – not everyone's favourite – but it was redeemed by the cheese board. I could do with a handbag-sized French-English culinary dictionary if one exists. (It does – I now have one – and subsequently the internet!) We didn't count but there must have been around forty cheeses on it. The waiter named them all but we took in only a few. At least we understood which were local, which were goaty or sheepish and noted the ones he said were strong or rich. We all had an assortment and ate too much. Dessert was a struggle and when petits fours arrived with the coffee, we groaned. We secreted away a couple for the next day. Breakfast would be an impossibility.

We were in Burgundy and didn't feel we could leave without buying some wine. But the car was full. Every corner of the boot was stuffed and opening it risked an explosion of dirty washing. We had a carefully constructed pile of 'stuff' between Barbara and Dave on the back seat. They could see each other but only just. I had a bag of bits and pieces by my feet. We had to find a little space somewhere.

'I think I can squeeze a box of six bottles on the floor by my feet,' was Barbara's contribution.

'Maybe I can too.'

I didn't think I'd be comfortable with so little wriggle room but I'd give it a go. Tony and I were interested in buying some *Crémant de Bourgogne*, a sparkling wine as good as many champagnes but not with the cachet of the name. I asked at reception for some advice regarding where to go. The receptionist produced a leaflet for a new tourist attraction called the Imaginarium. My first reaction was that it wouldn't be what we wanted. I was definitely into proper, local wine producers. But on closer reading, it seemed to suit our purpose. It was near the road we were taking, offered self-guided tours showing how the sparkling wine was produced and for a small fee included some tastings. And it opened at ten o'clock. Perfect timing.

It was a fun place. We sniffed the aromas that can be found in the wine from little puffers on the wall and tried our hands at turning bottles, part of the production process. None of us was good enough to get a job doing that. Some of the information was beyond our French but there was enough to keep us entertained. A friendly and knowledgeable young man provided us with several tastings, describing the wines in his beautifully accented English. The pink sparkling wine was a fresh summer drink; the white tasted like good champagne to me. Maybe I don't have a refined palate but at a third of the price of champagne, this suited me fine. The red sparkling wine didn't appeal. Red and sparkling don't go together. The final offering was an innovation in Burgundy, a lower-alcohol sparkling wine. It was sweeter than the others and aimed for a younger market. Our young man said it was selling well but I think I'll leave fizzy Ribena alone. We had to control ourselves as there really was a limit as to what we could squeeze in without leaving me behind. I love France, but it was time to go home.

A Bit of Pampering

The end of February and we were glad to be back in France again. Anna, Anders and the two grandchildren would be joining us in a couple of days so we couldn't spend too long on the downward journey. But we wanted to squeeze in a small stop. It now seems such a waste to pass through delightful areas and not appreciate them. A few years ago, Anna and Anders bought us a Christmas present of a row of vines in the Beaujolais area. This allowed us to buy wine from the estate at a privileged price and also to have special labelling done and join in events in the area such as helping with the *vendange* or grape harvest. Their choice had been clever as the Château de Pizay vineyard is only a half-hour's drive from our normal route to the Alps.

We visited Pizay for the first time two summers earlier. We arrived for our booked tour of the vineyard, expecting it to be the usual small group, but we were on our own. We had all the attention of the knowledgeable lady who guided us. The wine is made on the premises so there was no sending to a cooperative here. Our guide took samples from various barrels as we went round the cool, musty cellars and allowed us to taste the immature wine. I wished I had a better palate to appreciate all she was telling us. Back out into the sunshine, we wandered through the banqueting suite, often used for weddings. I could easily imagine how it would look with the bride and groom, the elegant tables, the flowers, the smart guests and of course, the local wine. The formal French garden with its hours of work keeping the topiary in shape would be ideal for the photographs. It was said to be a chess board and there were thirty-two 'pieces', yew trees clipped in stylised shapes like layered pyramids. I struggled to see how they fitted into a chessboard pattern but it didn't matter. We could still marvel at the delicacy of the work, and admire the elegant Jeanne de Marcilly, statuesque in the middle. We then went on the search for our own row of vines, a number in hand to find it. They all look exactly the same and we searched but failed to find the correct code. Some rows had lost their tickets or they were well hidden; ours must have been amongst them. A few tastings later and we had to be on our way but we decided we should return. The menu at the restaurant was tempting and we knew that the Château offered accommodation.

So that's where we were heading. A relaxed meal, an overnight stop and then on to Mottaret was the plan. We would hardly take longer than if we'd gone straight to our apartment. We were not in the main building but in a suite in more modern accommodation that also housed a de-luxe spa and swimming pool.

'Should have brought our swimming things.'

'I know. I meant to say but it slipped my mind.'

Our suite was well laid out with a lounge area on the ground floor and the bedroom on a mezzanine. We quickly unpacked our clothes for the evening and went out for a walk. A dilapidated gate led us into a vineyard. There was a wine walk marked by information boards so we followed them. I insisted on reading the French as well as the English as it was a good way to learn so I lagged behind. The flowery French read less well in English, even though it was properly translated. We Brits are not such flowery people. The vineyard, unusually, was flat rather than on a hillside and we could see a long way. The setting sun and still air gave the place an idyllic atmosphere. A few small hills were dotted around, the main one being the site of the Morgon cuvée de Py vineyard producing a wine that is one of Pizay's stars. We returned through the gate and circled the building to look at the outdoor swimming pool. It was heated. I dabbled my fingers in it and it felt lovely. This was more tempting than the spa pool but no swimsuit and now no time meant we needed to get changed for dinner.

The restaurant isn't large but the Château wasn't full. We were first to arrive at our table. I must learn the lesson that the French eat late as I hate being the only one eating. There's too much attention from the waiters. But others soon joined us and the ambiance improved. We chose the fixed menu. Although the wines of Beaujolais don't have the reputation of those of Bordeaux and Burgundy, we were not disappointed with our bottle of Morgon de Py. The chef's *amuse bouche*, a frothy concoction of I'm not sure what, slid down the throat enticingly and put us into the right mood for our terrine starter. I'd positioned myself so I had the best view of the other diners – nosiness is one of my skills – and was trying to identify what they had all chosen. There were some oddly assorted couples.

'The large guy looks really French. Did you notice how he chewed his wine when he was tasting it? I bet he's been here before. He has an air of knowing the place.'

'Why do you think he's French?'

'Just his air and clothes. And his general manner.'

At that point, he laughed loudly and indicated his agreement with his companion in a broad Yorkshire accent.

Wrong again! By the time the main course was on the table, I'd already eaten two bread rolls because they were so delicious. Getting through all the food was going to be difficult.

'Isn't it astonishing that you can feel so full when

none of the courses looks that large?'

When dessert arrived, I retracted my comment about the courses not looking large. It was a feast of chocolate in various guises which I loved but could not finish. Tony helped out. I'd just decided that I would not be eating anything at all the following day, and possibly not for a week, when a post-dessert delicacy arrived. More sweetness which I couldn't totally refuse but regretted afterwards.

We did skip breakfast the following morning, stopped at the shop to buy a few bottles and headed for the mountains.

The G & G Crêche

Our grandchildren, Maria and Lukas, were little ones back in 2007. As we get so much skiing, we gladly child-minded to allow their parents to ski together. If you live in Norway, as they do, the first choice has to be cross-country skiing but they love to get on the long runs and wide expanses, and the powder if possible, in the Alps. Anna, whose first love was slalom, has abandoned it in favour of telemark skiing and she and Anders, also a telemarker, are quite a feature on the slopes. You need to have good knees because of all the bending so I've never tried it. It looks fantastic when done well.

The little ones met cross-country skis early on, but we hired downhill skis for Maria when she was nearly four. The shop said that Lukas, at two, was too young. He wasn't one to be left out and we found him one morning, ready to go, with Maria's boots and helmet on, clad only in a nappy and underwear! So we let him have a try on a little slope (this time appropriately dressed) and he did remarkably well. When you bend your knees and your bum almost touches the snow, there's not far to fall. Just looking in the direction you want to go is enough to direct the body. How lucky they are!

A year on, and the abilities of the little two had increased. We all went up in the cabin to an easy slope. Anna was sorting out the reins for Lukas while Anders dealt with Maria. Reins are an excellent means of teaching children to ski, giving them some freedom while controlling the speed. A secure harness round the chest keeps the child safe and the length of the rein can be adjusted. Maria looked quizzically at the two of us.

'Are you taking Grandma on reins, Grandpa?'

'No, I think she can manage on her own now.'

Hanging on to the reins is hard work, I'm told. We were too scared to try. The children needed to have a go unaided so we came back down to the beginners' drag lift near the centre of Mottaret. They loved this, and were skiing well, Maria mastering snowploughing and stopping and Lukas being keener on jumping and crashing. At one point, I found Maria advising a teenager on how to grab the rope tow without falling. Oh, to have learned at that age! I was about thirty years too late.

While the children were going up and down by the drag lift, I thought it was a good opportunity to try out Joe's blades. Barbara had managed them, if briefly, but I'd never tried. They are excellent for teaching balance and getting the weight right. If you don't have your weight in the correct place, they oscillate from side to side uncontrollably. The first time Tony tried, I nearly wet myself laughing. I thought he was vibrating the blades intentionally and could not understand why he was doing it. He has mastered them now and even skied on them for a whole day. I wasn't keen on the idea but at least on the beginners' slope I could abandon them if necessary. They are okay, and I managed to conquer the vibration, but I can't see why anyone would choose them over a good pair of normal skis.

This year, the kids knew what they were coming to and were excited to be going to 'Grandma and Grandpa's little house in the mountains'. Several visits to their local slope had increased their skills further and even Lukas was showing signs of sense and an awareness that control was

113

necessary. We had bought them ski lessons for their Christmas present. We thought they would be in a small group but it was no longer half-term in France and they were the only ones enrolled. Of the options the ski school gave us, we chose to let them have three private lessons. Lukas, fearless physically, was not altogether enthusiastic about going off with someone he didn't know. But he was with Maria, and Alphonse was a likeable French guy who spoke good English. Seeing how well they could ski already, Alfie, as he told them to call him, was delighted to teach them.

'People will think I've taught these little people so well – just look how good they are! I will be in demand!'

It was successful. They enjoyed themselves and covered a lot of mountain in their classes. We were told to disappear – parents and grandparents weren't popular spectators. On one occasion, we needed to ski down Truite, the easy green run connecting Mottaret and Méribel, and one much used by the instructors when they set off with their classes. I decided we could nip by along the edge of the piste, unseen.

'Look! There's Grandma!'

Unseen? No chance.

Maria loved the lessons and talked frequently about Alfie; I think Lukas also enjoyed them and they improved in retrospect. She showed us many of the places he'd taken them, her sense of direction clearly not being inherited from me. Their skiing improved although just the practice of skiing around with us made them better. We devised 'blues only' routes, the run across the golf course in Méribel being popular. But the piste was boring; they had to go through the trees, over bumps ideally suited to their little skis, Anna bravely following. Lukas used every inch of piste in his quest for jumps.

The highlight of the week for them was going

through the Moon Park in Mottaret when they went over a series of proper jumps. They had seen the park from the lift and Anna asked them if they'd like to go over some of the jumps. Silly question. The drop into the park is fairly steep. Anders told them they must do big turns and not go too fast. We explored the rollers in the boarder cross area first but they were too tame. Lukas could barely get enough speed to get over them. That was a big disappointment, but the children had seen the proper jumps. As they set off towards them, Anna looked worried.

'They look a lot bigger from here than from the lift.'

She hurried after them to pick up the pieces, but there was no problem. They both succeeded in taking air and landing three jumps. Grandma and Grandpa took the easier route. Lukas then had his eye on the big kickers. They happened to be closed but at four years old, on 70cm Mickey Mouse skis, they would have been too much.

We'd been lucky with the weather and conditions were good for the children. Then the snow arrived. Visibility was poor and more than fifteen centimetres had fallen overnight. We were out early to ski the new snow, soft powder on a firm base, with more flakes falling. We loved it, and actually managed to ski it properly, a real achievement with our pathetic powder skills. But poor little Lukas struggled. He could make no headway, his short skis getting buried. He attempted the little rollers alongside the piste but even with Anna going first and trying to move some of the snow, it didn't work. Thigh-high snow was more than he could cope with. Maria, a bit taller and with longer skis, found it fun. But it was hard work and we retired to a restaurant for hot chocolate.

However, skiing is just a small part of entertaining the kids. What they find interesting is not always what you expect. When they first came to the Alps a couple of years previously, we asked them if they would like to go up in a bubble lift and, of course, this was a great idea. Best of all was going over the pylons when the cabin rattled around.

'Aaaahhhh'

Maria sang out as we went over the pylon and her voice wobbled. Lukas did the same.

'Come on, Grandma, you have to sing.'

So we all had to sing a note at each pylon. Fortunately, no one else was with us in the cabin as my singing is about as good as my sense of direction. Going on a 'bumpy lift' became a regular event and we planned entertaining routes for them.

'I can see Mamma down there.'

'Where?'

'There, in the red and white jacket.'

'I think Mamma and Pappa have gone somewhere else. I think they're in Val Thorens.'

'No, I can see Mamma just there.'

There was no arguing. Maria was always spotting Mamma – anyone in a red and white jacket. Her mother really moved around those mountains. We discovered that you can get all the way to Courchevel 1850 without skiing. An advantage of going down in a lift is that so few people do it, it's never crowded. For the children, there were two attractions in Courchevel, the roundabout and the crêpes. The roundabout is the traditional, small variety aimed at little ones. The price isn't small but you pay what you have to pay. Maria was especially keen on it. The crêpes with chocolate sauce went down well, and the grown-ups – we arranged to meet Anna and Anders there – were able to indulge in the favourite Grand Marnier variety. Coming back was a bit more difficult as we rode up in a full cable car. We had to hold the children as standing would not have been a pleasant experience, squashed in at crotch height.

'Can we go sledging today, Grandpa?'

This was another much-enjoyed activity. There is a

116

small children's area in Mottaret, well protected with straw bales, which is used for sledging. We bought two round sledges, like large tea-trays with handles cut out. These were lightweight so the children could carry them and hugely successful. The speed that the children gathered on them was astounding. That's why the straw bales were there. The other advantage of the round sledges is that you are so near the snow that it's easy to eat some. Maria dragged her hand as she came down, gathering snowballs and licking them.

'Maria, do you realise snow is dirty? People walk all over it and there might be dog wee or poo in it.'

No amount of reasoning made any difference. Snow was for eating. Tony decided that he'd take the scientific approach and explained to Maria that they would collect some snow in a glass, take it inside and watch it melt. She would then see all the dirt in it. This was duly done but Tony, unfortunately, paid too much attention to good scientific principles. He didn't cheat. The snow he collected turned out to be clean – and Maria continued to eat it.

Although our grandchildren are used to snow, it is still just as much fun for them as for English kids, of which Tony is an older version. He loves building snowmen so it's lucky the little ones want to join in. A gate leads from our terrace to the landscaped area around the building, ideal snowman terrain. There was much jumping on the mound that was to become the body in the course of construction. We eventually had a prize specimen, replete with carrot nose, pebble buttons, eyes and mouth, a scarf, and a dreadful black and yellow Mohican-style ski hat Tony had occasionally worn, one of Tim's cast-offs from his wilder days. It looked far better on the snowman. It was a sad day when we returned to the apartment after skiing to find that someone had stolen the hat and scarf. Tony particularly missed the hat. The snowman lasted for most of the season, getting slimmer and eventually headless as temperatures rose.

As a treat for the children, we said we'd all go out for a pizza. As Norwegians usually eat dinner between 4pm and 5pm, about the time Spaniards are finishing lunch, an early evening meal was nothing unusual. We went to Côte Brune in the middle of Mottaret. The pizzas were good. However, I did miss their old menu, not for the food on offer but for the translations. Restaurant menu translations are often odd, but here it was an art form. In fact, it was so clever, we wondered if it was deliberate. Where else was *jambon cru* called 'believable ham'? I should have tried the 'pork butcheries' and the 'melting part of lamb'. Not so sure about the 'tartar of ox (beef times)' or the 'hot toast of goat to honey'! The new owners cannot realise what a gem they have discarded.

As we left the restaurant, we heard music. The Highlights leaflet had advertised street musicians but we assumed the falling snow had kept them indoors. However, the weather hadn't stopped them and they positioned themselves under a covered walkway. They were five, a drummer, two saxophonists, a trumpeter and a guy encased in a sousaphone. Dressed in old-fashioned evening clothes, sad faces whitened, cheeks rouged, they played and mimed, a good French tradition. The children were fascinated and edged forward to get a good view. We all followed as they moved around the central shopping area. When the trumpeter made a play of trying and failing to collect money in his hat, Anders gave Maria a coin and she popped it in. The guy playing the sousaphone suddenly turned and played a loud, deep note right in front of her. She jumped and then laughed. He then went to serenade one of the girls sitting drinking under an awning, the serenade being the blowing of an enormously long note at the end of which he fell on the floor. The other four musicians waited a while, shrugged their shoulders, began to play again and moved off without him.

'Are they leaving him there, Grandma?'

Maria was worried but I explained that it was part of the performance. As we set off, I could see a waiter with a bucket of water. Whether it was poured over the recumbent musician, I don't know. Anna and Anders saw them all the following day in Méribel, dressed as clowns, singing and laughing as well as playing. Versatile performers.

Corduroy and Velvet

It was quiet after the family left, our little apartment suddenly bigger, tidier but not so lively. We were free agents with no one else to think about.

It was windy. There were billows of snow swirling around the apartment buildings. We shouldn't be surprised at how quickly the weather can change from day to day. Immediately after we went out, we needed our goggles just to see the way down the path to the ski lockers. The cleared path was covered with a depth of blown snow, just like a new fall, all the delicate, sparkling, flowery crystals smoothed away.

The blackboards by the lifts indicated that some of the tops were closed, but they still wished us *Bonne Journée* and told us which Saint's Day it was. I love the blackboards. They provide weather information, opening times, welcome messages, little poems, wise sayings and detailed drawings. There is a similarity in style between many of the blackboards, so maybe there is a Trois Vallées artist. The drawings are of animals – cows, a marmot, wild boar, deer, goats, even a St Bernard dog – and rural scenes of buildings, flowers and folk in local dress. Mont Vallon has a drawing of its mascot, a cow called Marguerite.

We skied in our valley, not having any choice, and visibility improved, the sun fighting its way through the clouds. As we went up Plattières, we could see the beautiful patterns made by the grooming machines overnight.

'Do you think the pisteurs ever take a lift up to admire their work?

We didn't know, but it would be such a shame if they never saw the sleek morning corduroy. We passed over the snow park, a collection of jumps, half-pipes, race tracks and boarder-cross runs, also beautifully prepared. We are not usually tempted but there was no one in it, so we had a go. There was an unexpectedly steep drop into the main bowl but no problem in such conditions and without other skiers. We looked at the jumps but a look was enough.

We thought we had chosen an easy option on our next run. Just too late, it became apparent that this wasn't a by-pass at all but the run-in to the boarder cross course and we were both already going at a rate. If I'd known where I was heading, I'd have been more prepared. The first bend was shallow, then the gradient increased sharply and we both got faster and faster. There were boarders rushing past on both sides, coming from nowhere, in spite of its narrowness. It was impossible to lose speed by turning and too dangerous a manoeuvre, anyway. The whole idea was to speed down a course like this. I managed another bend and by scuffing my edges slowed down enough to gain control. Tony had disappeared ahead of me. I emerged into the run-out, cross that he'd managed better than I had. I then spotted him a couple of metres above me on a rough snow mound. He'd been unable to slow down, had veered off the course and ended up on a pile of snow near the end of the course, skis wedged in, facing sideways-on. It took him several minutes to extract himself.

'That was a narrow escape. We could have got ourselves into a serious pile-up. I think we move on from here!'

While debating what to do next, the top section of the lift opened so we were able to go towards the Menuires valley. We were one of the first cabins to go up and there was a magnificent sight ahead of us. There wasn't a track marking the groomed snow in front of us, not a single groove or scuff. We moved rapidly across it, fearful in case someone should appear and spoil our pleasure. To the right was a piste heading down towards Menuires, untouched. We set off to enjoy the magical run. We stopped at the bottom, breathless, eager to go back up but knowing that no run could be better than the one we'd just done. We skied on down towards Les Menuires.

'Shall we have a go at the Boarder Cross we did last year?'

'Okay, but I don't know if I want to be videoed again.'

We went up the Becca slope and looked for the Boarder Cross running beside the piste. We found this last year and as we prepared to go down, we were asked by a young man if we wanted to be videoed. My instant response was, 'No', as I prefer not to see what I look like. However, it turned out he was a budding filmmaker employed by Toyota in an advertising campaign. He and colleagues were filming all comers who agreed and putting the footage on the internet – at no cost. So, we changed our mind. I skied down first, Tony followed with a borrowed helmet camera and the photographer followed him with another camera. A further photographer took shots part way down. It was a fun series of rollers and turns and felt faster than it looked on the internet. The video was password protected and we have omitted to give the password to our children!

This year, a bigger snow park had taken its place, and was attracting a large crowd of people, so we skied on by; it wasn't for us. This isn't our favourite resort although there is excellent skiing provided you don't look around much. It's not pretty.

The slope down towards the town was hard, icy and

crowded. I pitied the beginners struggling to overcome their fears as we and other skiers rushed past them. It's a dreadful place to learn. We were heading for the La Masse area. There are two excellent runs down from the lift here, a red to the right and a black to the left. The first time, many years ago, that we went up there, we were debating whether or not we could manage the black. We were in the cabin with a group of elderly, garrulous French skiers (well, they were probably the same age as we are now). When we reached the top, they all turned left. We looked at each other and Tony said, 'If they can do it, so can we!'

As they all turned into the restaurant, also on the left, we were shamed into skiing down the black. Today, the crowds were horrendous. The only lift with a moderate queue was the ancient two-man chair serving the Lac Noir slope. Anything was better than queuing so we took it, knowing the only way down was a black we couldn't see from where we were. At least we got a long rest before setting off. It was a field of moguls, not icy but polished. I could feel my heart thumping as I prepared myself. There were too many people; too many like me, tentative and needing space. But waiting didn't help because those setting off were replaced by others.

Seeing a good skier negotiate the first few moguls well, I followed him but found he was turning more rapidly than I could manage. I skidded on a polished patch and headed across the slope at speed. I was just getting back into control when I saw another skier, presumably having done a similar manoeuvre on the other side of the slope, hurtling towards me. To avoid the inevitable crash, I skied below her, gaining speed I didn't want. We brushed each other but both stayed on our skis. Just before I collided with a large mogul and fell head-first down the slope, I heard a shout as she hit someone else. One ski released and I slid down a long way before settling in a mound of soft snow at the side of the piste. I had snow everywhere. It filled my goggles and had gone up my right sleeve. I had lost a pole. I was shaken but everything seemed intact. I carefully felt my knees and they both worked. Tony had stopped a fair distance down the slope and was looking back towards me. I knew he was thinking of my past injuries; he always did if I had a spectacular fall. I waved to show I was alright and looked around for my missing bits of kit. A kind skier arrived with the ski and another with the pole for which I was immensely grateful. Climbing back up a slope is hard work and skiing this once was enough. I reassembled myself, taking my time to let my heart rate slow down and my breath come back. I de-snowed as well as I could. Getting the goggles clear was difficult. I found a dry tissue and wiped them, turning snow into wet smears. Much rubbing eventually gave me a lens I could see through and I skied cautiously down to join Tony.

'Did you hit your head? It looked as if you did.'

'No. I was lucky, but I jolted it.'

'You know, I think we'll have to take Anna's advice and get helmets.'

Helmets for many years belonged to children or ski racers. I was reluctant to wear one feeling sure they would be hot and uncomfortable. But the family were all moving in that direction and Anna's advice was sound. A few days later, we visited Christophe and made the purchases. I have been pleasantly surprised. The helmets are light and you hardly know they're there until you hit your head on something as you had forgotten about the helmet, or you have the inevitable itch on your head!

We'd had enough of crowded slopes so decided to head home. We queued. There were little groups of people chatting animatedly, others looking miserable and resigned. The noisiest were, as usual, the Italians, who seem to enjoy any situation, even queuing. A determined man wearing a bilious green jacket, elbows out, pushed his way past me, no doubt gaining satisfaction from the few metres he gained. I looked around at the assortment of ski clothing to pass the time. There were too many Rupert Bear checked trousers for my taste. As a ski bum, there is no uniform but inconspicuous seems sensible. We need to have credibility with our own children. Fairy wings and frilly net skirts are best left to the younger generation as are the more outlandish hats. Tony did on one occasion get a round of applause from a group of Germans when he decided to ski in a black hat with a large yellow Mohican-style plume, the hat later donated to our snowman.

Ahead of us, a group of young boarders were wearing their trouser straps dangling down rather than on their shoulders, a recent fashion statement. The straps carefully frame the buttocks but even if you think you still have a tight, neat pair, I suggest the shoulders are still a better place for the straps, especially at our age. Likewise, boarding trousers with the crotch just above knee height, and the belt practically under the bum is best avoided.

We don't buy new outfits each year, so the mode of the moment isn't for us. A good make that continues to look smart is a sound investment. Tony's interpretation of 'continues to look smart' has to be questioned occasionally as he does tend to wear ski clothes way beyond their sell-by date. He was the only man on the mountain in a green Spyder jacket and trousers for years. He reluctantly replaced them when he had to admit they'd ceased to be waterproof. One of our friends wrote in the visitors' book: 'Linda, throw away Tony's green suit. And while you're at it, throw away the duct-taped boots!' A snippet of advice, should you be an ex-racer. You do not need to prove it by wearing a catsuit – yes, we saw one! And don't borrow your son's T-shirt with 'Nice tuck, wanna f***' emblazoned on the back. Tony hasn't.

Something much beloved of older men is the one-piece suit. There was a faded one beside us, not enhanced by the beer belly its occupant sported. Although it may have advantages in keeping snow out when sliding down the mountain, a good jacket and trousers will work just as well (and hide the paunch better). I'm not a fan of one-piece suits for women either. They are a nightmare when going to the loo. You have to pull the whole garment down, negotiate the assorted layers underneath, hang on to the arms so they don't trail on the inevitably wet floor, also ensuring that you don't dangle a sleeve in the loo itself. This has to be done largely with one hand so that the other is free to find the loo paper and switch the light back on when the automatic timer turns it off. The time allowed is always just shorter than needed and the switch hard to find in the dark.

I am speaking from experience as I owned a shocking-pink one-piece in my earlier ski days in Norway. It was down-filled and cost far too much, even though bought in the sale. When I got it home, I decided it was too long in the body. There was a seam around the waist so I thought it would be easy to undo this, remove an inch or two and put it back together. Well, down is light and easily escapes. Tony was counting the money floating around the room and I had to resort to a scarf tied round my mouth to prevent my breathing in the contents of my ski suit. There is a limit to how far you can take 'internally warmed'. I got it back together and had many warm days skiing in it. The hassle at the loo, however, is probably the most abiding memory and the photos are reminiscent of the Michelin man.

I was forced out of my clothes review by a sudden surge forward by the crowd. It amused me to see that bilious green jacket was only two cabins ahead in spite of all his efforts. By the time we reached the top lift station, wind was blowing on the high peaks and the setting sun turned the curling snow into flames, the mountain top on fire. But there was no heat and we returned home.

Choose the Loos

Whether you are young or old, loos are important. Little ones have the advantage of using nature for their needs; we older folk prefer our privacy. The cold and enlarged prostates necessitate frequent visits so it's important to know where the good ones are. There's been something of a revolution in recent years in alpine toilets. They are more plentiful than they were and many have been recently refurbished. I think someone realised the old ones hardly helped to market the area. Many lift stations have basic loos at either the top or bottom. We don't expect too much from these but they work and answer a sometimes urgent need. The French have not changed in their attitude to Ladies and Gents. They do exist independently but there are frequent occasions when you go through the Gents to the Ladies or they are communal, with a few urinals on the side, as it were. Frenchmen have never been reticent in their peeing activities and can often be seen utilising the side of the piste, something Tony has also been forced to do at times. This is really more a function of poor planning than lack of facilities, but is accepted.

The best loos are associated with restaurants, naturally. However, not all mountain restaurants have plumbed water and the hole-in-the-ground variety is all that they can offer, with a seat sometimes, but primitive and often smelly. Some offer a roller towel rather than paper towels which rapidly becomes damp and disgusting, no doubt harbouring a lab's worth of bacteria. Coming out flapping wet hands isn't too good when it's minus ten degrees. Some restaurant loos are jealously guarded with notices warding off non-customers, so no peeing here unless you spend some money.

I decided to warm up my gloves on a really cold day at a Val Thorens loo by the bottom of the Funitel lift. I filled them with hot air at the hand drier. Unfortunately, I got them rather too close and burned the inside of both gloves. In my stupidity, I was busily burning the second glove before I noticed what I had done with the first one. The smell was a give-away. A bit of careful cutting later on removed the brown crispy bits of lining, so the gloves are wearable, if desperate, although they are past their best.

One loo I dislike is at the smart Chalet la Marine in Val Thorens. Going in the communal entrance used to give you a shock as you were confronted by a huge mirror hiding the urinals. Following refurbishment, this has changed but the mirror theme remains. The front and sides of each cubicle are mirrored so you can see yourself from every angle, not always a pretty sight.

Eco-friendly loos are popping up everywhere – or being dug out, perhaps I should say. It is a bit worrying when the little ones use them, perching on the edge of an inadequate seat. The thought of them descending down into the abyss isn't a comforting one.

Excuse me – I need the loo!

Slush and Marbles

Anne-Berit and Chris, our friends from Norway, had arrived. It's a long journey from Oslo, but they love the Alps and are as keen to cram in as much skiing as we are. We decided, as the sun was shining, to go to the fourth valley, the longest trip we could make. Yes, I know we were in the 'Three Valleys'. But there is a fourth – Orelle, beyond Val Thorens.

The view was worth the trip and we had beaten the rush. Mont Blanc was sitting above the surrounding peaks. No sign of any clouds on it, not even the little white hat it often wears, a good omen for the weather. The slopes were in full sunlight but it was cold enough for the snow to glisten without melting. We all shot down the first slope at full pelt, large giant slalom turns covering the distance down to the Rosaël lift and the restaurant.

'Is it a vin chaud now or shall we go to the top first?'

We decided we should earn our reward, so headed for the two lifts that go to the summit of Mt Bouchet. These are tediously slow but you can then say you have been to the highest point in the Trois Vallées at 3230m with its fantastic view (bizarre – as this is the fourth valley! No logic.) The two red pistes down from here are not always groomed but we were lucky today. Even so, the narrow part of Coraïa had grown considerable moguls and there was a group of people carefully surveying it. We skied past them, gaining admiring looks and hoping we were brave rather than foolish. It was easier than it looked. The main problem was navigating round the people.

'Don't forget to egg it at the end or it's a push up to the restaurant.'

We all tucked into the egg position, the heavier men having the advantage here. There was the inevitable plod for me. The restaurant called the Refuge du Plan Bouchet has a prime position facing the sun. It's always been basic but has recently added a glass veranda at the side, a gesture towards modernisation. And it has a monopoly; there's nowhere else to go. You can even stay there as accommodation is available. We sat in the sunshine and savoured our drinks.

Later, returning on the lift back to Val Thorens, we looked down at the Pierre Lory route, a dotted piste on the map which means it's not patrolled.

'We should have a go at that off-piste route down there.'

I am tentative about going off-piste but it didn't look too difficult and Anne-Berit and Chris were keen.

'We won't have time today but we could do it tomorrow.'

'What do you think the crowds will be like for the cable car? It would be good to do it on such a lovely day.'

'Well, it's Saturday.'

Saturday is change-over day for most accommodation so the crowds are smaller, even taking into account day-trippers. The cable car goes up to the Cime de Caron. This is such a popular lift you can queue for a seriously long time to get on it.

'Those straps are still there. They do worry me.'

'Doesn't stop you using it though.'

'No, but I always have a good look at them.'

There have been temporary straps on the top construction where the cable car arrives for several years, presumably to hold parts of it in place, something that concerns the engineer in the family.

Anne-Berit looked at the people scattered around eating their lunches.

'Should have brought a picnic.'

That's what most Norwegians would have done. When we first skied, in Norway in the eighties, everyone made a picnic lunch and took it with them, eating it in the restaurant at the bottom of the slopes. With a family of three hungry children, it made money go further. This was totally accepted and so it was a shock to us when we skied in France to find that such behaviour was actively discouraged. The French want us to use their restaurants and struggle to understand why we would prefer to do anything else. In a way, although not financially, I can see their point. However, things are changing and picnic spots are appearing. There are two viewing platforms at the top and it's a marvellous picnic place but we'd not planned for this.

'So where now?'

We had some choices and several colours.

The black wore us out, a run that went on forever. A rest of sorts in the lift, still on our feet, was our only preparation for the red. Part way down it, we had another choice that I'd forgotten about. This is a black mogul slope, Cristaux, which loops off the red and rejoins it later. Anne-Berit is an excellent mogul skier, far better than Tony and me. Chris is no slouch either. Last time we'd been here, the nerves and the knees would not persuade me onto it. I couldn't chicken out in present company. I watched Anne-Berit neatly bouncing her way down the slope, double-poling where necessary and keeping up a lovely rhythm. I knew I couldn't match it but with a sudden swell of confidence due to the new skis, I followed her and skied top to bottom without stopping. Sheer stubbornness kept me going towards the end as that is the steepest part of the slope. Just when I felt really tired, the moguls got bigger. Style, such as it was, went out the window and I survived the last few metres. Tony was following, willing me to stop, but he's just as obstinate as I am and kept on going, too.

It was fish soup for lunch in a handy restaurant, although quite where the fish came from when we were high in the mountains was a question we ignored. It tasted fine and no one was ill afterwards. We made our way home, never admitting that it was the last run of the day; we don't have last runs. That's when accidents happen.

The following day, we made picnics ready for our adventure on the Pierre Lory trail and set off early. It takes a while to get to the start. We had to get up high, right by the glacier above Val Thorens. We could see the blue ice of the glacier, beautiful and forbidding. There were tracks across to the left and tiny specks of people were moving higher and higher, aiming to get to untouched snow and create their own first tracks. We were not going that way; that was for braver, fitter, more able and possibly more foolhardy folk. To the right were other tracks and we could see a few people scattered along the long, uphill stretch that went to the highest point where you drop down into the fourth valley and the Pierre Lory route.

We followed in the indentations made by others, the snow being deep on either side. It was hard work. Going uphill on downhill skis is never fun but it was the only way to get to this part of the valley. It got steeper past half way and we took our skis off and carried them, heavy weights making our progress even slower. I debated removing some clothes but it was too much effort and I would only have to carry them. The compensation was the view. It was beautiful up here, the air still, the snow expanses vast and pristine.

'I hope this is worth it!' I shouted to the others, not knowing if they could hear me as we were spread out, each going at an independent pace.

It was a good feeling to get to the top. We gathered together to chat, get our breath and mop up the sweat. There is a short, steepish drop from the top then it's gentler. The conditions were spring-like, with the snow crusty on top. I skied with Anne-Berit, the men following. I was managing well and feeling pleased with myself. Tony was muttering to himself, cross that for once I was coping better than he was. Our intention was to take our time and find a good spot for our picnic. There weren't many people so we had the luxury of choice. We'd got about half way through the valley when Anne-Berit stopped and we all joined her. I thought it was picnic time, but no.

'I need the loo. I really, really need the loo!'

So plans were changed. We didn't realise we could move so fast in those conditions but we had to so as to avoid her embarrassment. She didn't want to provide a floor show for the lift above. We later found a picnic spot elsewhere. The trip was worth doing once. Not sure I'm tempted to repeat it as the ski down wasn't really worth the uphill struggle.

The following day, Tim joined us for the morning. He was coaching the English Alpine Squad in the area and had a couple of hours free. It's fun to ski with him; everyone raises their game and goes faster although competing with him isn't on the cards. He is simply the fastest and best in the family. He has managed 122 km/hr using Joe's GPS device, although he had to get up early to get hard pistes and few people. He even dragged Jessi, his long-suffering girlfriend (now wife), out of bed to act as sentry for him on a key bend so he knew it was clear. Competition runs deep in our family. We followed him around various slopes, staying in the Méribel valley so he could scoot off back to work when he needed to. He gave us a few tips, just one each so we didn't get too disheartened. I needed to look further ahead, Tony had to stop rushing his turns and Chris needed to keep his bottom in.

'You have your own style and you're safe,' was his verdict on his parents' skiing. Not sure if that's a compliment, but I expect it's accurate.

We were skiing back into Mottaret, enjoying the good condition of the piste that we rarely ski in the morning. It's usually the end of the day, with bad light and moguls to contend with. I was bringing up the rear and came over a lip to see Anne-Berit and Chris lying on the snow at the side of the piste, their skis, poles and legs in a tangled mess, Tim standing beside them.

'What happened?'

'Chris and I were waiting here when Anne-Berit came over the lip, hit a hidden patch of ice and was thrown backwards. I jumped out of the way, but Chris stayed put, knowing that Anne-Berit can always stop. This time she didn't and hit him.'

They got to their feet and were dusting off the snow when Anne-Berit tried to put weight on her left leg and shouted. We couldn't see what the problem was but there was definitely a problem. Memories of my own ski injuries came back, knee ligaments damaged five times and a lower leg break. The frustration of not being on the slopes when everyone else was out skiing, then the rehabilitation and nervousness. I hoped she wouldn't be in that situation.

'I can't put any weight on it'

'I'll ski down to the lift and get a blood wagon sent up.'

'No, I think I can ski on one ski.'

With Chris carrying the redundant ski, Anne-Berit got to the bottom of the slope in one piece, even managing to do it with some elegance. She was lucky not to be on a blood-wagon. I don't recommend this means of transport, based on an experience in Courchevel a few years previously. It's very bumpy and windy, you can't see where you are going and it doesn't help that you are in pain. The Cabinet Médical in Mottaret is close to the bottom of the piste and they went straight there. She had broken her tibia low down below the top of her boot and was duly plastered. The medical service was swift and efficient, issuing receipts, notes for the doctor back home, instructions on what to do and not to do, prescriptions for the pharmacy and claim forms for the insurance company so Chris carried an armful of paperwork back with him.

Back in the apartment, we had to sort out how to make the invalid comfortable. She and Chris were sleeping in the bunk beds in the second bedroom. As there are three on top of each other, there is less headroom than two-tier bunks provide and Vic had affectionately named them coffins. They're comfortable but not if you have a leg in plaster. So we swapped beds and they took our double in the main bedroom. Chris set about the long palaver of getting her home. Not the best end to a ski holiday.

'You always stop. That's why I didn't move. I didn't expect you to use me as a buffer.'

'Nor did I!'

Trips and Treats

Tony was looking through a little book he'd picked up at the Tourist Office called *Schuss à Table*. It was a gastronomic guide to the three valleys. It included a restaurant in Moûtiers, somewhere we'd never eaten. Moûtiers has an attractive, old area but otherwise doesn't have much to recommend it, the industrial areas sending a brown fug into the atmosphere that can be seen from the summits, a dirty blanket below the fresh, clean air. The restaurant, La Passerelle, in the old town looked appealing.

'Digging the car out is a pain, so we need to make it worthwhile if we do it. The forecast is good for several days, so we'll let the sun do most of the work. If we free the car tomorrow afternoon, we could drive down to Moûtiers, get a load of shopping and then eat there.'

We arrived at the restaurant just before eight o'clock and there was no one in it.

'I hate being first in. Let's have a walk around.'

We were the only people out; it was deserted. But it was interesting to see what else the area had to offer. There was another restaurant with an interesting menu but it was in darkness. A third restaurant looked inviting but was also empty.

'Which shall we go to?'

'Let's stick with the original plan. I think the desserts are better there.'

What Tony actually meant was tarte tatin was on the menu. We'd run out of places to look at so returned to the Passerelle. Monsieur, the owner, welcomed us and asked if we'd booked. We hadn't but clearly it wasn't a problem; the place was still empty. One of the fixed menus appealed so we placed our order. As driving restricted what we could drink, we had a half bottle of a Savoie wine we'd not previously tried, a Roussette, the house recommendation. It was pleasant and we settled down to enjoy ourselves. The chef's 'amuse bouche' and the starter were delicious, then the main course arrived. We'd both ordered the same, a veal dish with vegetables, which arrived in attractive, red pots, miniature casseroles. This didn't taste like veal. I had a feeling we were eating offal of some kind and I knew Tony wasn't keen on such innards. But I said nothing. Neither of us finished our meal.

'Did you enjoy that?'

'Not the most exciting meal I've ever had.'

I wondered what had gone wrong. We had the tarte tatin, an apricot version, for dessert, a coffee and then set off for home. When we got in, I grabbed the dictionary. As suspected, my French had let me down.

'It wasn't veal. *Ris de veau* is sweetbreads. We have just dined on pancreas.'

'Yuk! I knew there was something odd about the meat. The texture was too soft.'

It was probably beautifully cooked but neither of us felt too well. The thought of what we had eaten was not good for the digestion. That's one bit of French I won't forget. It's on many menus, often an expensive item, and probably something of a local and fashionable delicacy.

The following morning we were on the road early, heading for Val d'Isère. This was the second part of Tony's digging-the-car-out plan. Our Three Valley season tickets allowed us two days' skiing in the Espace Killy (Val d'Isère/Tignes). All the traffic was coming up the mountain, the workforce of the resort starting its day. We'd skied in Val d'Isère years ago and stayed many times in Tignes when Tim was racing in the British Championships there, so it was a nostalgic trip. I'd phoned the Tourist office the previous day to check the weather forecast – good all day. A couple of hours driving through pleasant villages in the morning sunshine and we saw the large dam indicating we were approaching Tignes. We turned where the road split to drive up to the first part of Val d'Isère, La Daille, recognising the strange, spiky apartment blocks at the foot of the pistes. There were people everywhere carrying skis, waiting for buses and being busy. There wasn't an obvious parking place so we drove on, the resort straggling along the road towards Val d'Isère 1850.

'This seems so big after Mottaret. Hope all these crowds don't mean busy slopes.'

Parking and ski passes sorted, we joined the queue for the Funival, a sloping train that goes through a tunnel in the mountain to the top. We crammed in like London tube train commuters, but noisier and friendlier. The average age seemed lower than in the three valleys, but that was fine. I have delusions of youth. We all spilled out at the top and spread over the wide expanses of snow. We needn't have worried about the crowds. There was adequate space for all. It was strange not knowing our way around but good to be somewhere different, out of our comfort zone for once. The mountains felt closer here than in our valley and were spectacular in the sunshine. No wonder the Espace Killy is advertised as the most beautiful ski area in the world.

'Are we going to have time to ski in Tignes too?'

'Not sure. Probably not but we'll see how it goes.'

The two resorts are linked but there was plenty of ground to cover where we were.

'We'll do a few runs, then do the Face, then have a

vin chaud.'

The Face, or the Face de Bellevarde to give it its full name, is a famous downhill slope, created for the 1992 Winter Olympics. I had vivid memories of being frozen to the spot years ago, stuck on a large mogul, fear making me unable to move for some considerable time. Today, I felt some of the same apprehension as we approached it, the easy run-in fooling the unwary. But it was in good condition and although undoubtedly challenging, it didn't stop me moving. For a black, it's enormously wide which is fortunate as it was the busiest slope we'd skied. I envied those who skied it with style. To think that racers go straight down the slope at full speed is daunting. They have my respect.

We felt we'd earned our vin chaud and sat in deck chairs at one of the mountain restaurants to enjoy the view and watch the people. It was warm but probably not warm enough to strip to the waist as a couple of guys had done. I didn't object; they added to the pleasant scenery. Amongst the many English voices, I could hear an animated French lady behind me, waving her elegant hands as she spoke, the rings on each finger sparking. She undid her fur jacket to benefit from the rays. She wasn't there for the skiing. Maybe she was a refugee from Courchevel. A couple of boarders almost wearing baggy trousers prepared to go down the mountain. How the trousers stayed up, I couldn't imagine.

'I think that vin chaud was stronger than usual. I've got VC legs and even my arms are wobbly.'

'Good job we did the Face first then!'

Tony had a glance at the map and we set off for an easy blue. As we arrived, a pisteur pulled a cordon across the slope to close it. The obvious alternative was a nearby black run called *L'Epaule*, the shoulder.

'We'll do this, then.'

'It's black and we've no idea what it's like.'

'It'll be okay.'

Tony's confidence was high, a combination of having skied the Face and a strong vin chaud. He scooted off so I had to follow. Although the first part wasn't steep, there were moguls. They looked as if they'd been there a long time.

'Must be years since this was pisted. I don't like the look of this.'

Tony laughed. 'Too late to worry now. We'll manage.'

Then the pitch got steeper, mogul after mogul. We survived the first drop, survival being the appropriate description. When it got steeper still, I regretted the vin chaud. My legs were not cooperating but I had to get down. I saw Tony doing a couple of long traverses in order to lose height. This was chickening out, but what the hell, I'd be a chicken. I looked around me. I was one of a small flock. We got to the final run out to find we had to push to get back to a lift. If we weren't sufficiently hot and sticky from the exertions on the piste, the final struggle ensured we sweated out the last drop of moisture we could spare. That was one difficult black slope. For the rest of the day it would be easy runs.

It was lunch time. We'd taken a picnic as the weather was good and assumed there'd be somewhere to eat it. But there were no picnic tables. We found a small brick hut with a doorstep and sat there.

'Mmm. I could do with removing my boots and giving my toes a breather.'

Tony was debating how to do this without getting snowy feet when he hit on the idea of using his helmet. His helmet is 'Large' and his feet are only size six, but it was a struggle to fit them both in. He looked pleadingly at my helmet so I gave in. I have a photo of him with a foot in each helmet. It comes into the same category as sitting on a beach with a knotted hanky on your head.

We remembered a strange lift that goes over a ridge, half of the journey being up and half being down, so headed there. It serves no pistes alongside, being a two-way transport. Travelling downwards on a chair lift is a weird experience.

'Barbara wouldn't like this,' Tony said, 'and I'm not mad keen myself.'

The weather on the way up was warm and sunny with no breeze. As we crossed the ridge, we entered a different day. A blast of air chilled us as the wind got up. I pulled my goggles down over my sunglasses. The snow beneath us was blown into crags and shelves. Sometimes it looked like the beach, with wave marks of the receding tide frozen into place; in other areas, like fish scales, nature's sculptures. Lower down, we could see raised patterns where skiers had passed over new snow days ago. What were originally grooves made by skis were now raised pathways, the compressed snow under the ski bases being all that remained. We got off the lift and put on our neck pieces to keep warm.

'Well, now we're here, we might as well ski a bit.'

We had no choice but to turn into the wind. Snow blew around our feet so we could hardly see the surface. Turning wasn't necessary as speed was impossible. In fact, we had to go straight to move at all. The upper lifts were closed. A couple of runs and we returned to normality on the more pleasant side of the mountain.

***

All season we'd been promising ourselves a really good lunch on the mountain. We needed a dull day when we would not miss good skiing and the weather gods had heard

142

us. The morning after the Val d'Isère trip, it was overcast, flat light with the occasional flake of snow.

'Now's our opportunity. We either go out and eat or not bother skiing at all.'

I knew exactly which option to go for.

'I fancy the Chalet de la Marine.'

'Trouble is, it's a long ski home from Val Thorens. Full of food and wine, that's not a pleasant prospect.'

'Well, we'll just have to manage if that's where we want to eat. We can take it slowly.'

The downstairs café at Chalet de la Marine is a frequent lunch or drinks stop and on one occasion we'd popped upstairs to have a look at the restaurant. It was delightful with a fire burning in the open fireplace and a fantastic array of desserts on a table just inside the door. I had trouble extracting Tony from the place. He is continually doing a one-man survey of all the restaurants to find out where the best tarts are. The current contender for the winning spot is La Casserole in Courchevel with Côte 2000 on the way back to Mottaret close behind. However, with regard to Tony's first love, tarte tatin, the vote goes to the Chalet des Neiges above Les Menuires. It's not only excellent: the portions are large enough to serve four. We usually order a single portion and several extra spoons. Chalet de la Marine might be a contender and that was one of the reasons Tony wanted to go there.

We hadn't bothered to book. It wasn't a day that would bring the crowds out. Arriving at one o'clock, we were shocked to see that almost every table was full. They managed to find one for us, although the people arriving twenty minutes later were turned away. Tony asked the waiter if they were always as busy.

'This isn't busy. When we use the terrace on a fine day, we can serve lunch to two hundred people.'

The bustle and activity added to the atmosphere and

143

we settled down to choose our meal. They offered a *Formule*, a two-course menu that appealed to us. We had *Joue de Boeuf*, beef cheeks. I was a little wary after my *ris de veau* mistake, but no problem this time. The quantity would have served a family of four but we had a valiant attempt at it. I regretted having tucked into the bread and dip that had arrived first. For dessert, there was a choice of either cheese or the dessert buffet. The waiter recommended the latter and it looked splendid, an array of around ten home-made temptations. Why else did we come here?

'Do you think I could ask for two small slices rather than one big one?'

We waited by the buffet for a waitress to serve us and explained that we were having the Formule.

'You can have a selection of three pieces.'

Tony was in heaven. He chose his assortment with care, expecting finger pieces. The waitress was in generous mood and we both received three large slices. Tony's tarte tatin was only just smaller than a full portion on its own. But it was the last slice and presumably not worth dividing. We sat down with our gargantuan helpings and wondered how we could possibly eat them. We couldn't, but we had a mighty good attempt. I have to record that for the first time in his life – and probably the only time – Tony left some tarte tatin.

Skiing home was interesting. Normally, I try to get a bit of bounce into my skiing. Today I made every effort to move my body as little as possible. It is surprisingly difficult to do. Luckily, the sun made an appearance so we didn't have to contend with hitting unseen bumps, an event that might have regurgitated my entire lunch. As our chair lift sailed over the last of Val Thorens, we could see a group of young men clad only in underpants and skis gathering by one of the restaurants. This was Friday, last skiing day for many holidaymakers. No doubt the result of a drunken dare the previous night, they were bravely preparing to ski down the mountain in the chill air. I twisted round to get a better look at their antics. Tony shook his head.

'In this temperature, there won't be much to see!'

With relief, we reached home and both headed for a sofa and collapsed. We didn't do much for the rest of the day.

The snow was getting variable. It was spring, warm sunshine, blue skies with just the occasional scribble of cloud. High up and early, the snow was still wonderful and stayed that way all day. But lower down, as it softened during the day, it piled into uncomfortable lumps, knee-twistingly heavy to manage. Then overnight it froze again so that in the morning there were masses of rattling marbles to vibro-massage the legs. These were not my favourite conditions and Eeyore came out often with me. My knees ached, a legacy of my previous ski injuries, and I felt I was not skiing as well as earlier on in the season. The pistes were getting more crowded as Easter approached, full of folk who only ever saw the mountains through a sea of people and never experienced snow conditions that were constant all day. We were spoiled; it was time to go back to England.

We had one last day to ourselves. Tony picked up the skis from Christophe's, waxed and edged ready for next year. They felt great.

'I think we left them too long before having them prepped this time. They feel so much better. I can actually get an edge in!'

We planned on a long morning, returning before there was too much porridge to ski through. Val Thorens was the best bet. We took the Côte Brune chair lift and looked down on some intricate patterns in the snow. Someone – lots of people, it must have been – had stepped out patterns on an unskied, flattish area, making circular and geometric patterns. The regularity was stunning. How did they do it without a template? Usually, there were just animal tracks to see, drunken, random wanderings of unidentified nocturnal travellers. But this was a piece of snow art, perfect but temporary. We skied up high, glad that the interweaving masses, a community of ants in the centre, had not reached the higher pistes.

'Where shall we have our last vin chaud stop?'

'I think the Chalet Chauvière.'

This is a small, basic cabin with a spectacular view over the glacier, serving drinks in plastic cups. On a sunny day, it's a real sun trap and is an inviting, rustic, friendly place. It's not always open, wind and low temperatures not favouring deck chairs, and it was now getting windier. So we decided against it and skied to Caribou instead. They are proud of their vin chaud here, little blackboards showing off its ingredients: honey, cloves, ginger. It was good. The neat blackboard-writer also told us about delicious crêpes and desserts but we resisted. The run down from the restaurant was perfect. We had it to ourselves. It wasn't a main highway so we savoured it, a rare treat on a day close to Easter. We said goodbye to the ring of mountains around us, familiar but never failing to impress. The brown pall of Moûtiers muck was ever there but we had learned to ignore it and looked the other way.

We returned to our valley and took our familiar shortcut home along the 'cowsheds' route. These are old, protected buildings on the lower part of the slope that were probably used for cows in the past. It was easier for the tired legs and weary bodies that ten weeks' skiing produces.

Ending with a Flourish

We were going home. It would be good to be back in England although leaving our French home was a wrench, a complex of feelings, sadness in leaving the beautiful Alps but still a readiness to return. Tony had done his homework and was determined no part of our first season as ski bums would be a letdown.

Chablis was the first stop. Choosing where to go for a tasting was impossible, there being the usual profusion of caves and vineyards so we asked the advice of the Tourist office. They directed us to La Chablisienne, a cooperative wine producer. Apparently, one in three bottles of Chablis originates here. It didn't have the atmosphere of an independent, locally-run operation but it did offer an extensive range of tastings. I was overwhelmed with the choice and asked what we could taste.

'Whatever you like, Madame.'

We were able to select from Petit Chablis right through to a Grand Cru, via classic Chablis, Vieux Vignes, the bubbly Crémant and Premier Cru. The assistants opened and poured, opened and poured, there being no shortage of anything nor problems in opening fresh bottles. No one blinked when we asked to try not one but two Grand Cru wines. This was what they expected. We could probably have tried every one on the list. Other tasters came in and did the same. We did, of course, make a few purchases. We liked the relaxed ambience of Chablis, as well as the wine.

Tony's final treat for our last night was a magical castle, the Château d'Étoges near Épernay in the Champagne region. It was a magnificent seventeenth century building with huge walls and rounded towers, a real fortress. It sat in a wooded park and as we drove through it along the sweeping driveway, I couldn't believe we were staying there. Our bedroom was a world away from most hotel rooms with an enormously high ceiling, about six metres, and a canopied bed. At eight o'clock we went down to the elegant dining room. It made a change to wear a dress and feel smart. Ski-bumming is a casual life and much as I love it, I do enjoy the thrill of dressing up. A few of the tables were occupied and we were given one in the corner. As always, I sat where I could face into the room so I could see everyone else in the restaurant, what they were wearing and, more importantly, eating. The food was lovely and we drank Champagne with it – not the most expensive on the wine list, but a good recommendation from the sommelier. What else can you possibly drink in Champagne?

The following day was for wine tasting. All the famous names were around, plus numerous smaller Champagne houses. We decided we should visit one of the great Champagne domains, Pommery. The *caves*, kilometres of underground cellars which were chalk pits from Roman times, are spectacular. We followed the guide past hundreds, thousands of stored bottles and learned about the various sizes, jeroboams and methuselahs. We saw ancient bottles, their contents probably undrinkable and heard the long history of the place. Widows dominate the production of Champagne, strong women taking over the businesses from their dead husbands. Louise was one of these, her name being associated with some of the finer Pommery vintages. Maybe Veuve Cliquot had similar business sense. Although the whole enterprise is now commercial and less personal than our Burgundy visit, we enjoyed our champagne tastings. As Tony was driving, I have to admit to a wobbliness of the legs after our visit.

'Well, have you missed being at work?'

'I can honestly say I haven't.'

'I never believed you would.'

There were a few, strange work-related dreams when I hadn't really broken the ties and my brain was still in work mode, but they stopped. The joy of being in the mountains, the pleasure of being accountable to no one for our time, the company of family and friends and the skiing, the wonderful, rapturous thrill of moving over fresh snow more than compensated for the demands of work. It was a good season.

A Bummer's Summer

...and the living is easy

Even the most dedicated ski bum can only ski while there is snow. That leaves a chunk of year to do other activities and we will run out of life before we run out of places we want to see. We discovered the Alpine attractions of summer – a wonderful bonus as we bought our apartment with only skiing in mind. The Trois Vallées resorts are open in July and August although there is nothing to stop us going at any time of the year. Temperatures can reach over thirty degrees but we never rely on that. We have now visited in almost every month of the year. When the mountains are green and covered in wild flowers, it's hard to imagine them with snow. I still don't know when they look most lovely.

We decided on a trip from late July to the end of August, during the 'open' months, inviting some non-skiing friends to join us for a walking holiday. But this would be later on; we had two weeks on our own first. We arrived late afternoon at the Alpages.

'Well, there's no difficulty in finding a parking place!'

The reserved area for residents was empty, never known in the winter. Rosebay willow herb lined the path up to the front door, tall, spiky sentinels keeping watch. A weed in England but perfect here. We unloaded the car, a few provisions from England to supplement the smaller range available at this time of the year. We also had tins of paint and brushes. There's never much time for such activities in the winter and the apartment needed some refurbishment.

'I suppose we should wish for bad weather so we can get on with our decorating.'

'I never wish for bad weather. We'll fit it in somehow.'

After we'd unpacked and I was doing the necessary amount of nesting, Tony unwrapped and unchained our garden table and chairs which we had left in a corner of the terrace during the winter.

'Looks like our anti-theft device worked. Too much trouble for the casual thief to undo this lot! It's taking me forever to get everything sorted.'

Sadly, we had experienced theft before. Tony wrote in the Visitors' book, 'Hope the person who stole the BBQ gets food poisoning!'

'Well, we need them in case the sun shines tomorrow morning and we can breakfast there. When you're done, let's wander into Mottaret and see what's open.'

The whole place was bright with colourful flowers, tubs and window boxes. Geranium growers have a good market. A few shops, mostly selling ski equipment, were closed, their windows blinded with brown paper. But enough were open for there to be a summery atmosphere, racks of clothing outside, potential bargains to be snapped up. Not crowded but enough folk around. The predominant language was French; it was a French time of the year. The tennis courts were fully occupied, the quality of the facility exceeding the standards of the games being played by a long way. A new sand volley-ball court was popular. Little children drove bikes and pedal cars around the open area in front of the Tourist Office, a brisk rental trade going on. The bouncy castle and trampoline were busy, as was the small ski lift towing kids in go-carts up the slope. They drove in haphazard, bumpy fashion back down to join the queue again. A small motorbike race track had no one using it.

'Lukas would love that when he's a bit bigger.'

'Probably costs a fortune. I expect the price is what's keeping people away.'

We looked around to see what restaurants were open, fewer than in the winter. 'La Belle Savoie', a little place we pass every morning in the winter on our skis, had people sitting on its large, sunny terrace. We'd never eaten there but stopped to look at the menu.

'I thought it just did snacks and crêpes. Didn't realise it was open in the evenings.'

'Let's go there this evening. We rarely go out on the day we arrive so it'd be different.'

A couple of hours later, we walked across the terrace, choosing to eat inside even though there were large patio heaters. The air cools quickly on alpine evenings. A charming French lady showed us to one of the half-dozen tables. Although the menu was small, the food was tasty and beautifully presented. Our hostess was the owner and we chatted in French. When I decided against a dessert, although Tony was having a slice of the inevitable tart, she presented me with a small sorbet, so I wouldn't be left out.

'A little touch like this is what will make us come back here.'

Some other guests arrived and we heard our hostess calling *'Depêche-toi! Depêche-toi, Tosca!'* As I turned to look, she dragged a large black dog from under the table by the door to make room for the latest arrivals. Tosca wasn't keen on the procedure but a few yanks on her collar succeeded in sliding her the required distance. Madame explained she was a Newfoundlander. Although old, sixteen years, she swims regularly in the lake using her webbed feet. Amazing what you learn when you think you have simply gone out for dinner.

155

We headed back, but instead of going to the apartment, went on past towards the Lac de Tueda for the pleasure of a walk around the lake in the dark. Once away from the buildings, a matter of ten minutes or so, there is no light pollution. Tonight the stars were clear and the silence loud. The full moon cast huge, sharp shadows, as clear as those on a sunny day. These giants preceded us as we rounded the lake and made our way home again, the romance of the walk only marred by the security lights at the small lakeside restaurant. We had no torch and needed none. The ground was dry and the moon was our searchlight.

Exertion and Relaxation

As I hoped, the sun reached our terrace around nine o'clock the following morning. It was warm enough to sit out and bright enough to need sunglasses.

'This is just bliss. I can't think of a better way to start the day than eating French bread and Beaufort in the sunshine, with a view of Mont Vallon. Just need the coffee to make it perfection.'

On cue, the smell of fresh coffee wafted out towards me as Tony carried the cafetière.

'I think this is even better than getting evening sunshine.'

We made our picnic lunches ready for the day's walk. We were going to the Refuge du Saut. This is a round trip of about four hours, just over two to get there and rather less to get back. A good walk we often do on the day after our arrival if the weather is fine as it is relatively short and allows us to acclimatise to the altitude. We walked past the lake, already with a scattering of people sitting by it and a few men fly-fishing. They whisked their rods in the air, the graceful curls of the lines settling on the water. The little hut selling cheese had a few people buying, the price reasonable. Nearby were hens, pigs and calves, a jumbled smallholding. We went up the steepish climb along a zigzag path.

'I think it's time to admire the view.'

We were both puffing badly. Walking takes more acclimatisation than skiing and we were feeling the thinner air even though we had not yet reached 2000m. Admiring the view was no hardship, however, and we could see the lake below us with the path snaking round it, miniature people dotted about. Higher up, we could see the lift stations, Plattières an empty shell, lonely without its skiers. I looked for wild raspberries, sweet fruit we had picked and eaten on previous walks here, but it was too early. Mid-August was the best time. An hour's walking and we had reached a plateau alongside L'Aiguille du Fruit, a craggy, scree-covered mountain to the left of the path. It dominated the landscape, a 'real mountain' according to Tony with its impressive points and steep sides. A zigzag path runs down alongside the scree, a route we have walked in both directions and doubly worn ourselves out. It was worth it for the rewarding ridge walk at the top. The stream ran alongside us, grey with glacial debris. We could hear the high-pitched squawking of marmots, brave sentries warning each other of the arrival of strangers. We scanned the rocks to see where their guard stood but their camouflage was too good. A flash of movement showed the rear end of an animal disappearing into a burrow.

An elderly French gentleman on his steady way down stopped me. Pointing at my walking sandals, sturdy but with open toes, he admonished me for wearing inappropriate footwear. Unfortunately, I understood what he said. Beware of the *cailloux*, the stones, he explained, pointing his stout stick at a large example. I should wear proper boots. His were of the ancient leather type, probably as worn by his father and grandfather and came well up his calves. I explained that in this warm, dry weather, I preferred lighter footwear.

He was unimpressed. He glared fiercely from under the rim of his crumpled, dusty hat and ignored my defence.

At my age, I'm not accustomed to being told off by random Frenchmen but from his vantage point, maybe I looked young enough to be put in my place. After several more serious words, and favourable noises towards my husband's sensible boots, we parted with a smile and a nod, although it was more of a shake of the head on his part.

We continued upwards, Tony's comments about walking like a dressage horse being excessive, I thought. The going was easy across the plateau, then a short climb to bring the Refuge into view. This is a place where walkers can stay overnight, a basic, comfortable place, recently refurbished. We walked round the building to the tables set out in the sunshine, occupied by a few other walkers and horse riders who had arrived before us. The horses were corralled in a cordoned-off area nearby, grazing, saddles off.

'Wine or hot chocolate?'

'I think wine. I love their chocolate but it's too hot today. A small carafe of the house white will slip down nicely.'

Although we had our picnics with us, Tony couldn't resist ordering a slice of tart. The prices are comparable to those down in the valley and actually cheaper than in some places. While waiting for the wine, I popped into their new loo, a non-chemical, ecologically friendly throne a few metres away from the Refuge itself. A big improvement on its smelly predecessor. Coming back, I could see people pointing to the hillside behind me and focusing their binoculars. There was a group of chamois moving across the slope, unbothered by the distant, human presence. The horses, on the other hand, were distinctly upset by their riders trying to catch them. The grass up here must be greener and they were enjoying it. They were eventually saddled and dutifully carried their riders back down the mountain. Other walkers were approaching the Refuge from the far side, returning from the direction of the glacier of

Gébroulaz. The time we walked there, a round trip of eight hours, we knew we'd had exercise. It was in that direction that we'd seen our first ibex. We were picnicking when an excited Frenchman rushed towards us shouting, *'Bouquetin, bouquetin!'* and pointed round the bend in the path. We had no idea what he was talking about but followed him to find three elegant ibex on a crag silhouetted against the skyline. It was a superb sight and we learned a new French word.

The time came to return and we faced the challenge of coming downhill without slipping, a harder task than climbing. The Frenchman's cailloux acted as marbles underfoot and caused sudden spurts of speed. I had a few slips, telling myself I'd have been no safer in boots.

'Why didn't we bring our poles? Coming down is so much easier with them.'

Walking poles were new to us, a Christmas present from Anna and Anders. I resisted them initially, feeling it was a concession to old age, but they are used by walkers of all ages. We keep forgetting them but we'll learn. A small sparkling stream was running down on our left, clear as a cliché, to join the faster moving grey one that descended all the way down the mountain to become the Doron river; we crossed it to return on the far side, a longer route but it meant we could give ourselves a treat and dabble our feet in the gaspingly cold water.

'I'm not sure I can take too much of this!'

The cold became painful but for a short while, it was deliciously refreshing. Near the end of our walk, we passed the elderly French gentleman sitting on a rock attending to a blister on his foot. I said nothing but made sure I picked my feet up well.

A couple of cyclists on mountain bikes went by, pedalling hard.

'Don't you fancy having a go? We could hire bikes for just half a day. We needn't go far.'

I shook my head. My bottom and a bike saddle have never been good friends and I had no desire to rekindle the relationship. Tony loves cycling and has fond memories of miles covered as a youth. Our kids had hired bikes in previous years and enjoyed it, usually taking the lift up the mountain and cycling down like lunatics. On Tim's advice, Anna and Anders cycled from Saulire into Courchevel. Unfortunately, there was a misunderstanding and they took a far steeper route than he recommended. A battered pair returned with makeshift bandages made from a torn-up T-shirt covering their wounds. Tony borrowed one of the bikes and took the lift half way to Saulire and cycled back down to Mottaret. It was a white-knuckle ride but he made it. Although he enjoyed it, we all decided it wasn't for me. However, that didn't stop Tony from trying to persuade me to do some more modest cycling. His proposal to cycle arose regularly, always turned down by me.

'I suppose I could think about it.'

The weather on the following day was miserable and wet so the bike suggestion was temporarily shelved. Although the forecast was for brighter periods later, we opted for a drive out rather than walking. But first we stopped in Méribel as it was their *braderie*. The main street was filled with stalls selling local produce such as dried sausages and cheese. Sports stores were selling off remaining stock at good reductions. All the resorts have such days and hope for sunshine to pull in the crowds. Unlucky Méribel, but there were still plenty of people around. Tony headed for a large stand of gloves, forever searching for the ultimate warm pair, or just feeding his glove fetish. I have no idea how many pairs he possesses, but he managed to buy one more. I bought three dried sausages, herby turds according to Tony who dislikes them.

We continued our journey in the direction of Albertville, Conflans being the destination. We'd visited this medieval, walled town before but had got both the weather and timing wrong. It was wet and closed for lunch. When the rain became torrential, we wrote it off as a mistake. However, we saw enough to make us want to go back in better conditions.

The sun came out as we arrived and we enjoyed the narrow streets and pretty little places selling local wares and souvenirs. One place was a real discovery. Called Atelier Cléofées, it was run by a husband and wife team, both artists. They produce watercolours and paintings in other media, a wide range of silver jewellery and collectables. We bought a small, framed ink-on-paper painting of Conflans for the apartment for the grand sum of twenty euros. With it, we were handed a sheet of paper outlining the lives and activities of the two owners. The variety of places they had lived, worked and exhibited made an interesting story. They are unusual people, talented and charming.

Lunch time was approaching and although shops were closing, restaurants were filling up. We chose a restaurant in the main square called Le Conflarain. Their savoury waffles were delicious. However, Conflans is a place where it rains. Although it had been warm and sunny, suddenly the weather changed and we had to make a run for the car. Maybe third time lucky?

I couldn't avoid the mountain biking much longer. Having not given a definite 'no', Tony took this to mean 'yes' and the next fine day saw us looking at bikes to hire. Tony sorted one for himself and a helmet in no time. I sat on the one offered to me, a more decrepit version of the one Tony was astride.

'This feels too big. Can I try a smaller one?'

The shop guy insisted it was the correct size for me.

'A smaller one would be a child's bike. You need a proper mountain bike. Believe me, this is fine.'

So we rented the two bikes for the morning and

cycled off towards the lake. The small incline up to the lakeside was a problem as I couldn't change gear.

'Let me have a look. Get off the bike and I'll show you what to do.'

Not being a cyclist, gears are a mystery. I could, as a child, manage the old Sturmey-Archer variety which I'd have preferred, to Tony's amusement. But it seems they no longer exist. He patiently showed me what to do and I tried but they were so stiff I couldn't move them. Tony put me in what he thought would be the best gear, whatever that was, and I stayed there. I managed to cycle round the lake as it was flat, the major achievement of the day.

'You're getting the hang of it. Shall we try to go up one of the paths?'

'Okay, but choose a shallow one.'

There were no shallow paths. Any sort of incline was impossible and I did more pushing than riding. I had to jump off the bike frequently and large red weals were developing on the inside of my thighs as I scraped against the saddle on each dismount. The bike was too big. Tony managed okay with his but it was clear this expedition was failing. After one particularly frustrating attempt to get going, I hit a tree root and almost fell, bursting into tears. Although we had hired the bikes for half a day, after an hour or so we returned them. I haven't been tempted again, although as Tony says, a good bike of the right size may be a different proposition.

'I did try, you know. I'm really cross it was such a disaster.'

C'est la vie! It turned out that the bike I was persuaded to hire was the smallest the rental guy had. We returned to the centre of Mottaret to watch the boules, or *pétanque*, competition that was in full swing. Pitches were everywhere; this was serious business for the French. I nursed my bruises at home.

163

We were watching the weather forecasts carefully. We needed two consecutive days of fine weather for the special walk we planned to do, a walk to Tignes and back over the mountains. High pressure in the area was in our favour and so, armed with ruck-sacks containing lunch and the minimum amount of clothing and toiletries required for an overnight stay, we set off. We had to drive to the start, a little place called Champagny en haut, about forty-five minutes from Mottaret. The sun shone for us.

'I hope the forecast is accurate. This could be unpleasant if it changes.'

The walk was spectacular. We could see the Grande Casse and the Grande Motte ahead of us, their tops still snowy. 'Grande' was an apt name. We'd not booked anywhere to stay in Tignes as we'd left the choice of day to the last minute. Fortunately, I had reception on my mobile and phoned the Tignes Tourist Board on the way. They gave me a couple of names of hotels. It wasn't difficult to book a night in a small place. After several hours walking, we approached the highest point, the Col du Palet. There was snow as far as we could see. The path was no longer visible.

'Wow, I wasn't expecting this. I'm glad someone else has already been here and we can follow the footprints.'

'That's a dodgy thing to do. They might have been lost!'

That was true and in fact some of the footprints went down to a Refuge we could see in the distance and not in the direction we wanted. Tony had a GPS device with him, however, so there was no danger and soon we could see the path again. Tignes appeared and about six hours after setting off, we arrived at our destination. The hotel was adequate and unpretentious. Dressing for dinner that evening meant zipping in the bottom half of our trouser legs.

We needed an easy day after our exertions to Tignes and back and there was the laundry to be done. Oh bliss! I am no more excited about a laundry visit in the summer than in the winter but it's less traumatic as there are fewer folk using the laverie. Afterwards, to raise our spirits, we had an indulgent, downhill-only walk. The Plan de l'Homme lift was running in Méribel, so we used our season passes, valid in the summer as well as the winter, to ride to the top and then walk back down to Mottaret. It was strange riding over the 'Bosses' slope and seeing it covered in flowers, a mass of purplish-pink and yellow where there is a tumble of skiers in winter. Within a short time of setting off, we noticed that the Arpasson mountain restaurant, near the Tougnète middle station, was open. We looked at each other.

'We've not really done enough walking to have earned a rest.'

'No, but I do like to encourage these places to stay open in the summer. I think we should give them some custom.'

A half-litre *pichet* of rosé wine was on offer for eight euros. What can you do? We spent a pleasant hour soaking up the atmosphere, the sunshine and the wine. On the way back we passed a wooden sign pointing to a small track to the right of the main path indicating 'Méribel 15 min'.

'It might be more pleasant through the woods. Let's go this way.'

'I can't believe it's only fifteen minutes, but you never know.'

The track became rougher and as I turned a bend I saw a youth coming up on all-fours. I began to wonder how difficult this track was going to be. I was obliged to admit that walking sandals, although comfortable, aren't always the best in difficult terrain. We negotiated the steep bit of track and came to another signpost, 'Méribel 15 min'.

'We've walked for fifteen minutes since the last signpost! I think the guy positioning the signposts had an evil sense of humour.'

A further half-hour brought us to Méribel, proving the point. Good job we were well lubricated with wine. And I had completely forgotten the trials of the laundry.

Winter in August

Our friends, Carol and Neville, were due to arrive. We'd arranged to meet them from the train in Moûtiers.

'Where else can we go? Don't really want to spend time in Moûtiers. Can we call in somewhere on the way?

'How about Brides? Haven't been there for ages.'

We have a soft spot for it because of the little *pensionat* where we stayed when apartment hunting. It is a spa town, much beloved by large French ladies of the mature variety coming for a *'cure'* – a confusing French word as it means a thermal treatment at a spa. My memory was of a genteel place, rather reminiscent of a fading English seaside town. So I was surprised to see that some significant refurbishment had taken place and there was a new, vibrant air. Nevertheless, the 'cures' still dominate during the summer months. Many restaurants were offering a *menu diététique*, presumably lower calorie than the standard. There were plenty of takers. Shapeless dresses covering shapeful ladies were emerging from the beautifully kept gardens, rather like those in Bournemouth, in search of lunch.

'Let's go into L'Arcadie for something to eat. That would be nostalgic.'

We'd had our first ever *tartiflette* there when apartment-hunting, delicious and certainly not diététique. It had changed little. Tables were still reserved for regular diners, who leave their part-bottles of wine on the table. I assume they are allowed some alcohol; no self-respecting French woman would cut it out altogether, whatever the diet. Brides is also being marketed as a ski resort in winter as it has a lift that goes all the way up the valley to Méribel. However, it probably comes as a shock to many young skiers. It does not have a skiing ambiance like Méribel or Val Thorens. Its main advantage in the winter is cost. I do wonder if anyone goes back a second time, especially if nightlife is as important as skiing. But it's a good summer spot, and my favourite hairdresser, Hélène, has a salon there.

'Why don't I have my hair cut while I'm here? I wonder if Hélène could fit me in without an appointment.'

She could and I turned into Tony's French wife once more. They do have a different way with hair in France. The mayor of Courchevel was having his hair cut when I arrived so I was in good company.

Carol and Neville still recognised me even with the new hairstyle. This was their first visit to our apartment. We had plans for good walks we knew they would love, breakfasts in the sunshine, evening drinks on the landscaped area at the back of our building watching the sun go down behind the peaks and good meals in the evening. Well, we didn't fail in all of them; good meals were weather-independent. The alpine climate is fickle and sunny days in one week are no indication of what is to come. We breakfasted inside on our first morning, the grey cloud and cool temperatures not enticing us out. But it wasn't bad walking weather and we acclimatised them with a walk to the Refuge du Saut. Day two was greyer. Ever positive, we decided to take the Pas du Lac lift up to Saulire and walk along the ridge. As we rode up the mountain, it started to rain. These weren't little spots but steady, heavy outpourings from the sky. As we passed through the mid-station, the rain became thicker and landed with splats on the windows of the cabin. Carol laughed.

'This is great. You have to see the funny side of it.'

I was disappointed as this wasn't how we wanted to show them our beautiful mountains. They were determined to enjoy themselves and a snowstorm – it was snowing properly as we rose higher up – wasn't going to stop them. At the top, we put on our waterproofs, tightened our hoods and got out our gloves. The wind hit us as we emerged from the lift station. Tony produced his camera.

'I have to get a photograph of this. Summer holiday in the Alps!'

'Where do you want us?'

'Just there will do. The background is either grey mist or darker grey mist so it doesn't matter.'

The ridge walk was abandoned as too dangerous in the conditions so we followed the path down the mountain. We took our picnics home and ate them in the apartment with hot chocolate. The photo was superb – we looked like ghosts.

The weather cleared a little and the scenery around us was re-appearing.

'How difficult is that mountain to climb?'

We were planning what our next walk would be and Neville was looking at Mont Vallon.

'It's not all that difficult. The path winds its way up the mountain and isn't too steep, just long. The round trip takes around eight hours – we'd need good weather.'

As we can see this mountain from our apartment – and our apartment from the top of the mountain – it is special to us. Mont Vallon is really a pile of rocks and much work has been done on it to make it stable. For several summers, we've been unable to get to the top because of ongoing works; mist and snow have also prevented us from completing the climb. We have managed to get to the top lift station once. We were keen to have another go.

But it wasn't to be the Mont Vallon year. The weather just wasn't sufficiently stable.

'Let's plan something we know we can do. Where shall we go to tonight to eat? Where can you recommend?'

The choice was smaller than in the winter but once out of the resorts, the restaurants were unaffected by seasonal closures.

'I know where we can go – Le Plantain!'

This newly refurbished restaurant had been much plugged by local radio during the winter. It's on the road from Méribel Village to La Tania, so not within walking distance. We had eaten here once before, several years ago, in the summer. It was a Frenchman's restaurant, basic and unpretentious, with workmen calling in for their evening meal of *diots*, the local sausages. We had a *brasserade*. This was something new and we weren't sure what to expect. It turned out to be a homemade contraption like a mini barbecue that was placed on our table. We cooked our meat on it. Regulating the temperature was impossible. The whole restaurant became hotter and hotter and all windows were opened. Other diners fanned themselves and we rather regretted the earlier decision not to eat outside. We did enjoy it and have never found anything like it anywhere else. So returning to the Plantain seemed a good idea.

Well, it really had been refurbished! It was beautifully fitted out with lots of interesting bits and pieces around the place. The menu looked excellent. There was no brasserade in sight. We arrived too early, as usual. When will we learn? But it filled up and the atmosphere was lively, the staff attentive, the food good and the wine copious. Their special starter of ceps, a local mushroom gathered on a nearby slope that day, was magnificent. The remains of the extremely large bottle Neville had bought came home with us.

It was their last full day. Finally, the blue sky appeared and the sun came out. We'd left it too late to do Mont Vallon so Tony had another plan. We drove around to Méribel, past the little airport with the small planes of rich visitors coming in low overhead, and parked near the golf course. Its condition looked immaculate, the snow it sits under for months and the many pairs of skis that go over it doing it no harm. We stopped to watch a golfer take his shot as we walked through the trees bordering the course. The easy going got steeper when we took a left turn to go up the Pic Noir ski slope. We stopped often to get our breath and admire the surrounding peaks.

'This is how it should be. I'm so glad we've got a proper walking day at last.'

'Don't worry. We like to see the mountains in all their moods.'

After an hour or so we were alongside the black Tétras piste. The path crossed it and turned into a series of zigzags, the only way to get up the gradient. I put my hands in the air.

'Why are you doing that?'

'My hands are swollen. It often happens at altitude. Just helping the blood run back!'

'Well, you should have remembered your poles. They keep the hands a bit higher.'

It was true, but too late to remedy now. Forgotten again.

'It's harder and slower walking up a black slope than skiing down it!'

'For you, maybe!'

We reached the plateau at the top where the silent chair lifts rested. This was Col de la Loze, one of the links between the valleys of Méribel and Courchevel. The restaurant, Le Roc Tania, was open, the terrace set with tables and chairs. The guy running it welcomed us like old friends. He wore a cowboy hat, a flamboyant checked shirt and a personality to match. We like this place in the winter with its cosy atmosphere, good service and extensive menu. Its summer ambiance was different but equally good. The deck chairs called us and we felt we had earned our rest before the homeward trek.

On the evening before their departure, we asked Carol and Neville to write in the guest book. They looked at comments other friends had made after summer visits.

'Survived another long walk and discovered you can get blisters on blisters.'

'Tony's "Bit of a climb" and a "Steepish descent" marginally understated reality.'

They agreed with both sentiments, the last in particular. We must become kinder to our friends. After some whispering, they retired to their bedroom with pen and paper, emerging about half an hour later. We now have a complete poem in the book, a unique contribution.

Their train was leaving from Moûtiers the following day, so we left a good hour before departure time, even though it's only a thirty-minute drive. They were just saying it was sad to be going when the weather was so good when Tony came up behind a huge lorry and trailer.

'Oh, no! I think the circus is leaving town.'

A circus, a regular visitor in the summer, had been in Méribel the previous week. We'd not taken much notice of it but now we had no choice. They had chosen today to move on, a procession of enormous vehicles carrying their equipment and animals. The winding road has one good overtaking place, otherwise it's risky, unless you are a local; they overtake anywhere. We got past the first lorry and a smaller one in front and moved on swiftly for a couple of minutes. Then we met the next instalment. The cavalcade had departed in a regular, spaced fashion, progressing with plodding splendour down the mountain. We looked at our watches.

'There's just nothing we can do. I can't overtake safely. Maybe as we get lower down and approach Moûtiers, they'll go a bit faster.'

'We were saying it's a shame to go – perhaps we'll be staying!'

Tony was thinking through contingencies.

'If you miss the train, there's a chance we might be able to drive to Chambéry and catch it there but it would be tight. Do you know when the next train is?'

'Not for several hours. We would miss our connections by a long way.'

And so we discussed the various possibilities and eventually got to Moûtiers. We turned off towards the station with two minutes in hand. Tony pulled up in an illegal parking place and the three of us leapt out almost before he had stopped. We rushed onto the platform and they got on the train as the doors were being closed. That was a bit of unanticipated excitement we could have done without.

Local Living

It might be considered laziness: we weren't walking every day. But we were doing other activities, finding out what happened locally and visiting places. There wasn't the need to drive ourselves to walk all the time, just as we didn't need to ski such long days in the winter. We were living here, not just visiting. We were still making the most of being in the mountains.

We'd seen a notice advertising the *Fête à Fanfoué* in Les Allues, the pretty, old-fashioned village just down the mountain from Mottaret. Although there is new development here, the main village is largely untouched, much as it has been for years. The fête is an annual event that has been going around thirty years, a real piece of Savoie. It takes place on a Sunday, starting with a mass and continues all day to the dance in the evening. We arrived early afternoon along with an abundance of local people; English voices were few. This was a local affair for local folk. The atmosphere was friendly and relaxed with the glorious sunny weather being a bonus. The ladies in their traditional black dresses may have found the weather too glorious. Everyone was out, all ages from babies to the elderly. Smart old ladies in their well-ironed, white blouses and neatly coiffed, permed hair accompanied tanned gentlemen, some in summer suits, others in shorts with socks and sandals. They looked their best. Mixed in were a few chic, typically French, younger women wearing impossibly high, backless shoes, but for the most part, it was casual holiday dress. The road was lined with stalls where local craftsmen sold their wares or demonstrated their crafts – everything from lace-making to the most elegant face-painting I've seen. We tried *bognètes*, local small cakes, hollow and deep fried, then covered in sugar. They were cooked on the spot, tasty mouthfuls, best eaten fresh.

Street entertainment was strictly French with a pair of bereted accordion players wearing red neck-scarves, black waistcoats and trousers, singing traditional songs. Their encouragement to dance was taken up by a few. As we sat on a low wall to watch, a Frenchman rushed up with two chairs for us. Visitors were welcome. As we watched, we drank wine – one of the best local Chignin we were told – from plastic cups. At two euros a time, we weren't complaining. A troupe of folk dancers performed on a makeshift stage further along the road. The slow, stately dances, again to accordion accompaniment, were delightful. Young girls and boys formed part of the troupe and had some dances of their own as well as joining the adults. It was a shame to see so few men dancing, just two in fact, with women taking the men's parts. The origin of the dances was explained to us and many had strong Savoie roots. One was called a bognète, the same as the cakes we had tried.

I wanted to buy a souvenir to support the local craftsmen. A lady in local dress showed me everything she had on the stall, eager to sell and to please.

'I'll buy something. I don't know what.'

I got a wooden heart to hang in the apartment. Not a work of art but a rustic reminder of a local event.

A wonderful aroma drew us to a large cauldron full of onion soup, a traditional dish to be served in the evening. But we had to leave. A pity to have missed it but all the

175

same, we felt we had really joined in a piece of local culture.

We were going to Le Praz in the Courchevel valley that evening. We went to watch the flying men, those who perform awesome feats, either self-propelled or with the help of a machine. The summer ski jumping was taking place. Competitors from around the world take part, leaping off the 120m jump and landing on watered, artificial grass, a green swathe looking like velvet. This was a free event with free parking and transport. We wandered in and found a spot on the tiered side of the arena. The jumpers seemed minute as they leapt into the air, brave, graceful bird-men. Watching the sport on television doesn't do it justice. Interspersed with the jumping was an aerial display by fighter jets in the totally blue sky. Two events requiring skill, precision and total focus.

It was more than an international competition. It was a celebration of the sport, with children from the Courchevel Club des Sports opening the event. They skied down the ski jump, a feat in itself for these little people, while the commentator told us their ages and the best distances each had jumped. It was hardly believable that a six-year-old lad had jumped seventeen metres. They carried flags representing the competing nations. We were amused to see the Union flag – it's a long time since Eddie the Eagle did his modest bit for us.

They told us the Courchevel Club des Sports was the best in France. We bought coffee, hot dogs and crêpes from the hard-working club volunteers, probably the parents of the budding jumpers, to support them. And there were air activities available to all in an adjacent field. Adventurous folk jumped from high platforms and trampolines onto huge airbags. How I wished I were younger!

***

176

The resorts had an end-of-season feel to them. As the last days of August approach, everything winds down. The shelves in the supermarket were getting increasingly bare.

'You know, I prefer to be here totally out of season than towards the end of it. Then you know everything will be closed and you have to go down the valley to shop. And I like the tranquillity.'

'I know what you mean. There is a strange 'limbo' feel to the place now.'

We had a few days left and one last visit to make. I wanted to take home some Beaufort and I thought that it would be satisfying to buy it from Beaufort itself. We drove to the Beaufortain mountains, the designated area where the 'AOC' cheese is made.

The *laitière* was open to visitors. We wandered through the cool, temperature-controlled cellars full of large, ripening rounds of cheese, a pleasant break from the hot sunshine outside.

'It's a bit smelly!'

'What do you expect? It's full of cheese!'

Tony used to be a soft cheese man, Brie being his preference. But Beaufort cheese is changing that. We liked the little, attractive town and had lunch sitting at a table on the pavement outside a small café. Afterwards, we went for a walk and saw the brown cows grazing in the distance.

'Just think, this is the grass that was eaten by these cows last year and their milk has turned into the cheese we've just bought!'

It's usual in the Alps to take mobile milking machines to the cows rather than bringing the cows down. We hadn't realised it was milking time and unknown to us, a mobile machine had been positioned behind us. Suddenly the quiet cows were heading for us at speed.

'What's happening?'

'Look behind us. They've spotted something we hadn't!'

A cow-line is much like a bee-line and we got out of the way.

We had one last set of visitors before our departure. Our son, Tim, and his wife, Jessi, were passing through on their way to Switzerland. It was hardly a direct route from England but it was an opportunity to spend a couple of days with us. They brought fun, good company and rain with them. We wandered down Truite, the easy green run in winter, to Méribel on a miserable day to have a look at the market and buy some *pain d'épices*. Well, we didn't go for that but there was good shelter by the stall selling it and we tasted so many samples that I felt an obligation. We drank hot chocolate in a bar and Tim bumped into someone he knew. He always does; skiing is a small world.

We had a good meal together before they left, as always with bubbles; Jessi likes to celebrate.

'You must look me in the eye when we toast,' she said.

'Why?'

'If you don't, it's seven years' bad sex!'

Couldn't risk that; no doubt the younger generation knows best.

***

It was a good way to finish the summer. We'd had all the family and good friends to share our adventure. Lifts were running for the final time and the remaining shops were closing, no one interested in the last few items on their shelves. As if to compensate for the miserable weather of the previous few days, the sun came out. The thermometer registered just six degrees outside the apartment when we got up but by the time the sun had reached our terrace, it was warm enough to sit out for breakfast.

'We ought to make the most of the chance to use the lifts for the last time and the weather is perfect for a high walk.'

Tony planned an up-and-down walk, a new one we'd not done previously. We would take the lift to Saulire, then the cable car down into the Courchevel valley. We'd then walk all the way back to Mottaret, stopping for a picnic somewhere.

We arrived at the lift to find the staff, always pleasant, in a particularly jovial mood. A cursory glance at our passes – no checking them on the machine today. They were preoccupied with laying a table alongside the lift station. I could see an unopened bottle of bubbly, a carton of raspberries and assorted other packages emerging from a supermarket bag. The end of the season was a time to celebrate. We reached the middle station where again, there was a table laden with goodies. Three lift employees were already sipping local white wine from plastic glasses.

'Hope there's no emergency today that requires a clear head!'

We got out at the top and waited for the cable car to arrive. There was a crowd of people already here, some on mountain bikes, others with climbing equipment, setting off for the *via ferrata* on Saulire, a pathway with fixed ropes, not a true climb but something described as providing *sensations fortes*! Tim had done this a few years before and his tales of overhanging rock had convinced us it wasn't for us. We'd make do with milder sensations. But for the brave, this was a perfect day. On the way down in the cable car, Tony and I were debating which of the steep routes joining the main piste was the Grand Couloir. The lift attendant who rode with us pointed it out. This is a black slope we've never skied. I would love to but I'm scared. Only recently has it been designated a slope – it used to be an off-piste route. It looked pretty steep even with no snow on it. Hmm.

At the lower cable car station, I could smell meat cooking. A portable barbecue was busy preparing lunch for the lift folk, one of them standing guard with a barbecue fork. I couldn't see any wine but I bet there was some.

We set off towards Lac Bleu, along a path designated *sentier découverte*, or discovery trail. It was steepish and winding with information boards every so often, good excuses for a rest. They provided little-known snippets and details about familiar places and events. We learned the Vizelle and Verdons cabins are garaged underground in summer to be less intrusive to the landscape, and that the Méribel and Courchevel valleys cannot agree on the name of the main peak on Saulire. What is the Dent de Burgin for folk in Méribel, is the Croix de Verdons in Courchevel. We looked across the valley to magnificent chalky stripes of rock, vertical protrusions, a different geology, a different landscape. The information board told us there was a path up there to the Dent du Villard.

'That would be a good walk. I bet there are a few precipitous edges on the way up! We've got one day left – let's do it tomorrow.'

We neared the lake where the path was just loose rocks and were glad, for once, we'd remembered our poles. The water was low but it was true to its name; it looked blue. Going over a hillock, we saw a recently laid bonfire, new wood ready to be lit.

'Maybe the end-of-season celebrations continue up here.'

We'd never know. The path continued to Col de la Loze where we decided to have our lunch. Ignoring the scattered picnic tables, we settled ourselves in the corner of the restaurant terrace, bare of its winter furniture. The season had already finished up here. It was a sun trap and we sat on our *sitte plater*, the folding polystyrene mats that were relics of Norway, to cushion our rears and protect ourselves from the splinters of the rough wood. After lunch, I lay down, my rucksack for a pillow, and closed my eyes.

'How is it you always just lie back and are instantly comfortable? I can never get into a good position. It's always the same, whether it's on grass or any other surface.'

'Maybe I'm less fussy or just better upholstered.'

Tony proceeded to wriggle around, worse than a dog settling down to sleep. He eventually stopped moaning in time for us to set off again. He had removed his boots, his foot problem not being confined to ski boots, and was now picking splinters out of his socks. Fortunately, I'd not been asked to rub his feet. We spent the rest of the walk planning our next one. The Dent du Villard appealed to both of us.

We arrived back at a ghost town. No signs of the celebrations remained. Everything was shut. But the sun still shone and we fell asleep in deck chairs by our apartment.

The following day, we drove to Lac de la Rosière where the Dent du Villard walk started. This was beyond Courchevel 1650, a town we'd not visited since our apartment-hunting days. It had grown, new wooden chalets dominating the original properties which still lurked in the background. There were several walks from the lake. Ours was designated difficult, a 750m climb estimated to take five hours for the round trip. The walk up was not for those who dislike edges and at times we skirted precipitous drops; a fall would have been the end of us, not only the end of the walk. But the path was well maintained and easy enough. We zigzagged upwards, turning at times on white, chalk rocks and looking down at landslips. At the point of one turn was a boulder with a large cross on it to prevent walkers continuing in the wrong direction. The path did continue but was like a narrow shelf across a bare cliff face. A foolhardy man would have gone that way. Near the top, the trees disappeared and we had panoramic views to glaciers on one side and down the valley on the other. Looking straight down the steep drop we could see hillocks and holes where water had eroded the rock, a weird white and green limestone landscape, our most spectacular walk.

'What a great way to finish our time out here!'

A scramble at the top brought us to the *Table d'Orientation* where we had a 360 degree view. We climbed down to a grassy spot for lunch, bread, cheese and ham. I lay down in the sun; Tony did a rather shorter wriggling manoeuvre than usual. The walk back was fast and we easily beat the predicted time, adding further to our satisfaction.

It was time to go back to our English home. This time we were heading for the Loire and the wine areas of Pouilly and Sancerre. We left our usual motorway route and drove through parts of rural France we'd not previously seen. The villages on the way were a mass of flowers with flower pots and troughs in any available space. Bright red geraniums dominated and we understood why so many places had a *village fleuri* sign. English villages are beautiful and I love them; French villages are different with a special charm. The brown-beige walls of the houses with the ubiquitous shutters, some smart, others with peeling paint, epitomise France for me. The tree surgeons in France must never be out of work as every village had its quota of pollarded trees. At first, I disliked them but they are so much part of the French scenery you have to accept them and ultimately see some beauty in their rounded, spiky heads. The lush rolling countryside was so much better than the flat, uninteresting views from the motorway. There are no tolls, either, and although progress is slower, that is one of the pleasures. As we approached Pouilly-sur-Loire, the trees bent across the narrow roads, their branches almost meeting. The sun shone through them making a striped pattern, the bright patches blinding our eyes.

As ever, there was too much choice in selecting a vineyard for a tasting. So we called in at the tourist agency in Pouilly for advice. This meant a lovely drive alongside the Loire, although the fact that the road surface where we stopped appeared to have tiny fragments of blue glass embedded in it was worrying. The tyres survived. We discovered that the various vine growers have special open days and we were directed to an appropriate one in the centre of town.

'How do you think we get in?'

We tried several doors but inexplicably and sadly none would open. So we took the second recommendation of a cooperative on the edge of the town. This was not such a grand affair as the Chablisienne in Chablis but we were able to taste and buy. Pouilly-Fumé is not the only wine produced in the area. Pouilly-sur-Loire is very drinkable if probably a poor relation of the more famous wine.

'Would you like to try our red wine?'

We had never heard of red wine from this region.

'Maybe there's an undiscovered gem here and they keep it all to themselves.'

We now realise red wine from this area is little known elsewhere for good reason. We did not buy any.

The Tourist agency guy also said there were a number of villages nearby that produced excellent Pouilly-Fumé, and he recommended a drive through them. This gave us a wide view over the surrounding countryside as they look down on the river. We stopped in the village of Les Loges whose whole life seemed to be wine production.

'We'll have to visit one of these places. We can't come to a village like this and just pass on through.'

So although we had not intended to visit another

cave, we did. The Domaine Pierre Marchand & Fils looked inviting and a smiling lady took us to the tasting area in a corner of their *caveau* where the wine was produced, bottled and labelled. This was a small, private producer, rather scornful of the cooperatives, and rightly so. Their wine was magnificent. The aroma was of delicate fruit and the taste grew as I swished it around my mouth. We regretted having already bought so much; we just had to buy a few bottles more. As we were leaving, the owner came in.

He insisted on taking the wine to our car for us. With his cap, braces and highly hitched-up trousers, his smile and graciousness, he completed a lovely visit. Maybe we'll avoid the cooperatives in future. They are safe but less interesting.

We then crossed the river heading north for Sancerre. The Loire was low, and where the water had retreated, sandbanks were exposed. These were beaches for the locals who were enjoying them. The area just across the river was unattractive but Sancerre itself is a small, pretty town on a hill. Wine production here is big business and the local people have worked hard to promote their product. There is a Maison des Sancerre, built by local growers to tell their history, which we visited. It is a new building amongst the old but fits in well. We restricted ourselves to a single visit: time and money were running out. Tony programmed our satnav, Henrietta, to find the vineyard as it was a little way out of town. She got us there – La Perrière. We walked into a cave, a real cave cut out of the rock face. I pulled my fleece around me as it was chilly. To one side was a museum of old wine-making artefacts and a room where a video was played in complicated French. Near the front of the cave were huge, shiny, stainless steel vats, new technology alongside the old. On the other side was a bottling plant. We were free to wander where we wanted.

'This is a lot different from the packaging lines I

worked with.'

To see a bottling plant in a cave with growth on the walls and rough rock underfoot was a world away from the packaging lines I managed in the pharmaceutical industry. But it worked for them. We tasted a few and liked them. Surprising ourselves, we bought some rosé, not our usual choice but a lovely summer wine. As for the white wine, I usually prefer Pouilly-Fumé over Sancerre, but now I'm not sure.

We needed to head off to our hotel for the night. Tony had not told me where we were staying as again he wanted it to be a surprise. It was. Château de La Verrerie was the closest to a fairy castle I have seen. With elaborate grounds and a large lake, it looks like something out of a children's story. Our room was grand with a huge, original fifteenth century fireplace and a vast ceiling. We ate in the Château's small restaurant in the grounds, called La Maison d'Hélène.

It didn't look special as we approached but it had a welcoming atmosphere, intimate and friendly. The three-course meal was perfect and, as we have usually found, reasonably priced. Part of the Château is open to visitors, a separate wing away from the hotel rooms, and a guided tour is free for all guests. We arrived at the appointed time the following morning to find we were the only ones taking the tour. We were in for a surprise. The whole visit was set up as a piece of theatre with two actresses, dressed in period costume, taking us from room to room and explaining the history of the place in well-rehearsed monologues. We discovered we were actually in what was once a part of Scotland! The land was given by Charles VII of France to the Stuart family in gratitude for their support against the English and remained in their hands until the nineteenth century. A family tree even showed a link to Princess Diana, no doubt pleasing English tourists. It is now the private home of Baron Béraud de Vogüé, as well as being a piece of France's heritage. While neither of us understood every word as it was, of course, in French, elaborate French at that, we both understood enough to follow and enjoy the story. We had reached a bit of the UK without even crossing the channel.

And Finally...

So were we better skiers after our season? We think we were. That's not bad, getting better as retirees. It might all be in the head, of course, as seeing a video of myself skiing is an experience I don't enjoy. So much in skiing is down to confidence so if we think we are better, that's all that matters. However, the most important thing was to enjoy it. And we did. This will be the pattern for years to come. Our ambition is to still be skiing at age seventy-five (it used to be seventy-two) when we qualify for a free ski pass! And we were fitter too, our summer exertions keeping our bodies moving. As we arrived home at the end of our winter and summer seasons, Tony looked at me thoughtfully.

'You know, you should write a book about this.'

Around Fifteen Years Later

Looking Back

Did we regret it – our investment in the Alps? Was it a waste of money? Did we keep the apartment or was it a matter of recouping our losses?

No regrets – far from it. We visited regularly, both summer and winter. But we had a problem. The family was growing. With eight adults and seven children, to say nothing of the dogs, we were seriously short of space in our two-bedroom apartment. If we used every bed, we could still only get seven people in – all sharing the single bathroom and loo. Family holidays weren't going to happen, or not in any comfort.

We debated whether we could afford to buy a bigger place.

'We don't have to stay in Mottaret. If we sell, we can leave this valley. We can choose a completely different ski resort, maybe one where the property is cheaper.'

There were decisions to make and money to be counted. So we went back to the process we used for our Millennium Project and listed all the pros and cons. But little had changed. We decided that we liked nowhere as much as the Three Valleys, nowhere as much as the Méribel valley and within that valley, nowhere as much as Mottaret. To add to that, we liked the Alpages development best of all. So we were back to where we started. There were bigger apartments in the five buildings comprising the Alpages but there were two major problems with them. They rarely came on the market and when they did, they were way beyond our means. This was depressing.

'I have a Plan B,' Tony said. 'Why don't we keep this apartment and buy another of a similar size in Alpages?'

It would have several advantages. No fees for selling, more space than we could ever afford in a single apartment. And... we could rent it out when we didn't need it. Wonderful idea! So we looked at the market. Even more depressing. Little for sale and the prices were higher than we thought they'd be.

I wondered about other buildings in Mottaret. A second apartment needed to be close but didn't have to be in the same chalet or next door. Some of the nearby buildings had properties for sale and we looked. Maybe a little smaller, maybe with a few issues – one had the kitchen torn out in a post-divorce rage. I was tempted with an attractive one up the hill but Tony insisted it was too far away.

'You know what our family is like. Someone will forget something and trips back and forth will take ages.'

But to me it seemed like our only hope of another property. We looked at it a second time. Tony insisted making an offer was a bad idea. We returned home with little hope of achieving our dream. A few weeks later, we were leaving our house when I noticed an envelope on the step, presumably dropped by the postman. It was from a Mottaret Estate Agent with details of an apartment for sale in Alpages. It looked like it was exactly what we wanted – but there was no price. I phoned up. It was more than we could afford – but not hugely more. An English family was selling it as they no longer wanted to ski.

We put in an offer and to our amazement, it was accepted. We bought the apartment blind. I didn't think I'd ever be brave enough to do that. But we knew what these apartments were like, their location and standard. This one was on the ground floor of the adjacent chalet, diagonally opposite our apartment. I asked the estate agent to walk me through it on the phone, describing everything. I expected some hype – it had been the show apartment for the building, everything was in excellent condition, nicely decorated. We could have gone out to view it but Tony was busy on a project for his old company and didn't have the time. At worst, we'd need to redecorate and replace some of the furniture. So we jumped in. And guess what? It needed redecorating and we replaced some of the furniture – but we saved the cost of a visit.

I often wonder if we'd have got our second apartment if that dropped envelope had blown away.

Problems weren't over, however. We agreed the price in May 2010, expecting to be the new owners well before the following winter. There were continual issues. Were the vendors leaving the rug? I didn't care but they debated it for ages. Then they wondered if their children would prefer them not to sell at all. But an apartment sitting unused for years didn't appeal and I expect they wanted the money. The third agreed date for the exchange of contracts eventually happened – in March of the following year. We never understood the delay but it no longer mattered. We had our second apartment. It was roughly the same size as the first but differently configured. And we could walk across the grassy (or snowy) area between the two. In fact, the children regarded that area as our garden and complained if anyone else walked along the path that crossed it. So English of them!

It was a perfect solution.

Getting Left Behind

Not only was the family getting larger, the youngsters were skiing better. We'd decided ski lessons were better Christmas presents than yet more toys so that became the norm for the grandchildren.

Maria and Lukas had been first, when they were around four or five, shortly after we retired. It was now the turn of Joe and Vic's little ones. Olly was the next to take lessons but he'd 'skied' before, when internally stowed. Vic discovered she was pregnant while staying with us as she did a pregnancy test in the apartment. She decided she would continue skiing, but carefully. The following day, Joe took us off-piste to ski in a gully. It was shaped like a half-pipe and wasn't difficult. Joe led the way, then Vic, then us. We were all enjoying the whooshing from side to side when we arrived at a flattened area, a road in summer. Tony and I stopped on it but Joe had already disappeared straight across it into the continuation of the gully, so Vic followed. Neither had realised there was a small but steep field of moguls just below the lip. Joe bounced around but survived; Vic buried the tip of a ski, cracking it, and worse, bent her little finger. Joe, who's a doctor, strapped her up and they managed to get back to the *Cabinet Médical* in our valley where she discovered she'd broken the bone. Undeterred and plastered, she skied on hired skis the following day. Olly arrived around eight months later, no worse for his early introduction to the hazards of skiing.

When he was one, Olly continued his skiing career. Joe and Vic had a backpack, a substantial baby carrier, and they decided to see how successful it would be for Joe to ski with Olly in it. The little one needed many layers of clothing and wasn't impressed with all the dressing. Once loaded into his carrier and strapped onto Joe, life improved significantly. He had an excellent view, warm in his multiple gloves and socks. His goggles protected most of his face and the large white pom-pom on his hat looked like a beacon as it bobbed up and down.

We chose easy slopes and more importantly, uncrowded ones. Joe is an excellent skier, but the hazard of other, less competent individuals is always present. Vic skied close behind them as a rear guard. Joe modified his skiing to take wider turns and make the ride as smooth as possible. Olly was quite a feature on the slopes. He grinned the whole time and clearly enjoyed the experience. The staff at the lifts were worried he'd be cold but Vic checked him regularly and it wasn't a problem. Sometimes Olly would fall asleep, quite comfortable next to his Daddy. When we got back to the apartment, and Vic removed the backpack from Joe with Olly still in it, the little one continued to rock from side to side, the pleasant motion of skiing staying with him.

When Olly's time came for proper skiing, we booked him into a group lesson but it turned out to be a class of two. He and the French lad had no common language, but got on well and parted at the end of the week with a hug. All classes end with awards – medals and certificates – so Jamie was keen when his turn came round. But the expected success didn't arrive in a hurry. The class with a stated maximum of six children, had eight beginners in it. There were two instructors and chaos ensued. There were never more than two children in an upright position at any one time and most were in tears. They were all little tots and it was a recipe for putting them off skiing for life. Joe and Vic removed Jamie before the class was half over and I went to the ski school to complain. We agreed, as a compromise, that Jamie could have a double private lesson. With a different instructor.

'That'll be good, Jamie, won't it? A nice instructor all to yourself.'

'No.'

'Don't you want to learn to ski?'

'I'll ski with Daddy on reins.' Being dragged around like a sack of potatoes was a more apt description.

'But don't you want to ski on your own like Olly?'

This received a scowl and a shake of the head. We had a problem. The following day, Vic asked me to take him to the lesson as there was a chance he might cling less to me than to her. Jamie held my hand and studied the snow.

'Look, Jamie, over there. It's your instructor, Philippe.'

'No.'

'Over there. Just by that big sign.'

'No.'

'He's smiling. I think he looks a nice man. Don't you?'

'No.'

Eyes rooted to the ground, he barely allowed me to haul him to his lesson.

Philippe turned out to be small and friendly with an easy manner, a suitable teacher for a three-year-old, but Jamie looked resolutely down. He didn't cry; but the tears that filled his eyes and the trembling bottom lip told me how near he was. The chocolate biscuit I passed to Philippe for later on in the lesson was the only point of interest.

I asked to stay for a while and that helped. Jamie skied down the small beginners' slope with Philippe skiing backwards, hanging on to his ski tips. There was a 'high five' at the end. I relaxed a little; Jamie was participating. They had a number of runs and then I told Jamie I was going back to collect my skis. He wasn't enthusiastic about my disappearance.

I took my time. When I returned, he was skiing unaided down the slope, slowly and carefully in a wide snowplough, and he could turn and stop. In my absence, there had been a few tears but he had tried his best. Afterwards, he said he didn't much like Philippe as he wouldn't go and find Mummy and Daddy for him.

But the following day, he was a different child, delighted at his new freedom. He set off with confidence on shallow slopes, in full control. He went over small bumps, took off – 'I did fly in the sky!' – and landed. He was skiing on his own. When we asked him if it was difficult he said, 'You just go this way and then go that way.' Skiing at its simplest. Clever Philippe had succeeded.

George, number three in line, went to the local Ski Nursery, Piou-Piou, from the age of three and adored it. In his last year, he particularly enjoyed the 'escapements' when one of the instructors took a few of the better skiers out onto bigger slopes. Wonderful for his confidence as he told us of his adventures. Now we're on to the last set of grandchildren. Idris went to Piou-Piou but best of all likes going fast with his Daddy. It's in the genes. Tim was a ski racer, after all.

Now, we have trouble keeping up. They handle evil conditions far better than we do, think falling over is great fun, go over every jump they can find, are not daunted when the visibility is down to a few metres and wonder why we are bringing up the rear. Maria has helped me down an unpisted slope I didn't mean to be on.

I wouldn't have it otherwise.

The Neighbours

Our Alpages neighbours had been in Mottaret longer than us. A stylish, French couple of our age from Provence, we'd said '*Bonjour*' on many occasions but it took years before we really became friends. She spoke no English, he understood a little and would grin and say, 'English weather!' when it rained but proper communication needed to be in French.

We invited them round for an apéritif, opening a good bottle of red wine and having an equally good white in the fridge. However, she was a rare beast – a French woman who didn't drink wine. Her only tipple was a rum cocktail she made herself, a recipe she'd picked up when on holiday in Réunion, and she came armed with a huge bottle, most of which she left with us. We've had a regular supply ever since. Fortunately, we like it. He drank whisky, insisting on the cheapest as he liked to drown it in soda. We had no soda so he popped back to get his own. He had to put up with our single malt; Tony winced.

We chatted comfortably, my French getting better when loosened with a drop of alcohol. However, there comes a point when fluency gets overtaken by memory loss. This is normally somewhere south of three glasses of wine. I speak English quickly and my tendency is to try to maintain the same rate in French. This adds to the disaster and errors tumble over each other. I cringe the next day but at the time it feels fine.

She was a fan of *'Oh, là-là!'* When excited, she would explode with a double dose, *'Oh, là-là, là-là!'* and shake a limp wrist at the same time. I became used to it and even found myself doing the same. Tony's French improved although I translated when a glazed look came over his face.

'Trouble is, by the time I've worked out what to say in French, the conversation has moved on,' he moaned.

We were invited back to dinner. Steak, barbecued on a snowy terrace and served with Provençal rosé wine. Fortunately, only the cooking happened outside. It seems rosé goes with everything in their part of the world. The red came later with the cheese (served before the dessert, naturally). The size of the kitchen in no way inhibited our friend's creations and if we didn't take large enough helpings, she would simply put more on our plates. A portion of crème caramel was put into a bowl for us to take home with us. It was midnight before we wobbled the short distance back to our apartment.

She would often ring our doorbell. Knowing of Tony's sweet tooth, she would bring a plate of *crêpes* (there was rum in her recipe – it went in everything) or another French delicacy for us to try. She would wander in wearing her pyjamas and give us hugs. We were her *petits amis anglais*.

Then came the shock. We'd said goodbye and *'A Bientôt'* to them at the end of January a few years back, having had yet another amicable, boozy meal together, knowing we'd see them in early March. But, by then, they had separated. We knew they weren't married but they'd been together many years. We weren't going to take sides. He is now happily married and she is happily on her own. They are both still our friends.

C'est la vie.

One day, 35 lifts, 4 tired legs

There had to be a challenge.

What gives you a thrill in the snow? Skiing a black slope full of moguls? Making fresh tracks in deep powder? Being the first down a perfectly groomed piste under a blue sky in the sunshine? Maybe all of them! It's the adrenaline rush all skiers know. But we decided on a different kind of test, one needing stamina and planning rather than bravado. And one we had a chance of completing!

We attempted to ski all the lifts in the Méribel valley in a day. We first tried this in our earlier days, succeeding the first time, failing the second then having another success. We were now older. Could we still do it? We set the criteria – which lifts were in scope and which weren't. Cheating, do I hear you say? Well, not really. We eliminated two beginners' 'magic carpets', the Stade lift in Méribel which isn't open to the public, and the transport lift from Brides les Bains. It still left thirty-five lifts – enough for us.

A mid-March, sunny day when most lifts are open until five o'clock chose itself.

Good weather is necessary and you need the longest possible time. Tony planned the route carefully. The total descent is fixed, the distance across the snow isn't. You can't make any lift go faster. On average, we had twelve and a half minutes per lift, to go up and ski down, with some contingency at the end.

We carried all our food as there'd be no time for restaurant stops – sandwiches for lunch, chocolate and chewy bars and, of course, water. Calories don't count on a challenge day. Lunch would be in a cabin – chair lifts invite you to drop anything not attached to you.

We started at the earliest opening lift. No one queues properly, of course; only the English know how to do that.

The gremlins are always out to get you. Lifts will open late, some will stop. We needed a Plan B. Trouble is, you don't know what Plan B looks like until something goes wrong.

'That's going to bugger us up!' is a much-used expression.

We always felt we were running late, mainly because we kept losing track of how many lifts we'd done. Counting to thirty-five can be difficult at our age!

Crud and slush at the end of the day are inevitable. There is no avoiding having to ski into Méribel four times – there are four lifts from there – and conditions deteriorate with each descent. However, rumours of trench foot from leaking ski boots are widely exaggerated.

When a ten-year-old French boy on a snowboard cuts you up, he will mutter 'Merde!' when you complain.

We skied the most economical way using minimum effort. There are no points for style (what is that?) And we always chose the easiest slope if there were alternatives. We synchronised loo visits (whether we both needed to go or not). Things get really bad around lift twenty-eight when the legs scream and the knees belong to someone else. Tony went quiet. When I asked him what he was thinking about, he replied, 'Our sofa'. I focused on a glass of Sancerre and a couple of ibuprofen. It takes superhuman strength to resist the allure of a deck chair. The year we failed to complete the challenge included a foolish deck chair stop. This time, we gave in to a hard wooden bench for ten minutes. We didn't expect to enjoy it all – but we did enjoy most of it. Especially the victory photo at the end*. We congratulated ourselves on the fact that we skied down a total height of 12,500m. That's nearly one and a half Everests and over eight times Ben Nevis! There were five minutes to spare at the end of the day. Not bad for Oldies.

(*The cover of this book shows my celebration at the end of the challenge!)

First Tracks

It sounded like a dream. First down the mountain on a beautifully prepared, empty piste, snow glistening in the early sunshine. The chance to own the mountain before all the punters came out.

But it wasn't. Méribel was offering an early morning ski followed by breakfast at the top of the mountain – an event called the *Matinale*. The cost was sixteen euros each so, of course, we signed up. It was scheduled for just a few mornings, weather permitting. A group of us gathered at the Roc de Fer lift to take us up to the top. The plan was to ski as much as possible before breakfast was served so we set off at a lick – to be pursued by a pisteur, waving his arms and shouting. Whoops! We weren't aware he had to go first for the sake of safety. There were two available pistes, a blue and a black, both of which we knew well. An untouched black slope in the sunshine, a mist of fine snow crystals sparkling in the clear air; I wasn't really bothered about breakfast!

A whole mountain with just a handful of skiers meant we were instantly spread out, no one else in sight. No one to keep clear of, no one to avoid, no one to be scared of, no one even to admire. Simply no one. We swooped down the slope, feeling like the best skiers in the world. We weren't, but who cares? Top to bottom with no stopping. We needed the ride on the chair lift back up to get our breath back.

But breakfast was welcome after a few fast runs. We had real Savoyarde fare – cheese, ham and salami, baguettes, croissants, pains au raisins. As much as we could eat. And local wine. Wine at breakfast! In addition, it turned out one of the group owned a vineyard in Sancerre and had brought along a few special bottles. Spoiled or what?

'How can they do this? It must cost a small fortune!'

I asked one of the food team and she said it was just for publicity and would never pay for itself. It needed many staff as well as the food. They had opened two lifts early to get us to the top of the mountain and there were several pisteurs plus assorted folk serving us. They could only handle around twenty participants and we were fewer than that.

'Wasn't there enough demand to run at capacity?'

'No. I don't think enough people heard about it.'

'Radio Méribel would publicise it.'

'Ah, but then we would have too many people!'

I remained confused but grateful. As the day got into action for the rest of the world, we remained at our tables, raising our wine glasses to toast passing skiers who had large question marks coming out of their heads. This wonderful event moved to a different lift a couple of years later from where we had the choice of four runs down, three reds and a blue. The pattern was the same – as much skiing as you could fit in before as much breakfast as you could consume. We took family and friends; it was a holiday highlight, whatever everyone's standard of skiing. I think we worried one set of skiing friends, Maggie and Stuart, by inviting them to join us at the Matinale the day after their arrival. No time to find their ski legs, no time to settle in. But they agreed – and what better way to start a skiing holiday than on an empty slope in perfect conditions? I can still see Stuart toasting passing skiers as he finished his breakfast with a wide grin on his face.

Then it stopped. We didn't discover why but assumed money had run out. A year or two later, the restaurant on one of the peaks proposed an early breakfast plus a single run down – at a price. It had become a commercial proposition, less fun, more people and much more expensive. So we decided against it.

Then a new resort director was appointed and he decided he needed to do something special for the property owners, restaurateurs and shopkeepers in the valley. He re-introduced the Matinale. Breakfast (minus wine, but you can't have everything) was now in a restaurant rather than at the rustic mountain-top tables and we had less time for skiing – but, hey, it was free! It ran successfully several times throughout the winter season and we could not believe our luck. But it lasted one year only. We are dubiously optimistic it may return yet again.

If it was good enough for Josephine...

… Beauharnais, that is, Napoleon's wife, it should be good enough for me. Always on the lookout for somewhere interesting to stay on our many journeys through France, we'd found Château de la Ferté Beauharnais in the *Bienvenue au Château* guidebook. No one had confirmed my reservation, so I hoped they expected us. Finding the place was the first issue. Henrietta, our Satnav, eventually triumphed in spite of her French being of the Ted Heath variety, but worse. We reached the village of La Ferté Beauharnais – and then left it within seconds. I re-read the minimal instructions.

'It says it's in the centre of town.'

'You might have told me sooner. I saw an impressive building off to the left.'

Returning slowly, we saw closed gates with 'Château Beauharnais' on a small plaque.

'How do we get in?'

I consulted the instructions again.

'Ah, it says the entrance and parking are opposite the village hall. I should have spotted that before.'

As we drove yet again past the gates, we noticed a sign pointing to a small road we'd passed at least four times, opposite the *Mairie*. Finally, we arrived in front of a seriously impressive, centuries-old building.

'This will do nicely!'

We walked up the grand central steps to an open French door. No one was around so we made the random choice of left and wandered down a corridor lined with unusual artwork. A knock on a door brought us confused attention from a gentleman we supposed was the owner, Daniel. Yes, we were expected but he seemed unsure what to do with us. Hitting on the idea of showing us how to use the code on the side door, he gave a detailed explanation of what to do when it didn't work. Ominous. He indicated we should follow him to our room. We were in the Blue Room on the first floor of one of the two towers. Apart from the novelty of being round, it boasted a large four-poster bed with beautiful white linen and a mohair blanket. Elsewhere were pieces of period furniture, a large fireplace, a pair of riding boots and some elegant hats. I wondered who had worn them, whose feet had trodden the oak boards and who had gazed out of the shuttered windows over the lawn to the driveway and gates.

I asked Daniel about places to eat. The guidebook had mentioned a local restaurant. I hoped it wasn't the one I'd spotted with a closure notice – *Congé annuel* – on the door.

'There's a good *auberge* very near, but it's closed for the holidays. I can recommend another place but it might not be open tonight. Shall I phone and find out? I could book a table for you.'

While we were waiting for the result of his kind offer, Tony decided to have a shower.

'There aren't any towels! Well, there's one hand towel.'

'He'll be back in a minute. I'll ask him.'

Fifteen minutes later, I decided I'd better go looking. Tony couldn't wait and had decided he'd manage with the hand towel.

'Take the key as I'll be in the shower.'

'Where is the key?'

'Probably in the door.'

There was no key; there wasn't even a lock.

I found our host who seemed to have forgotten all about our need for a restaurant. But no problem, he said. All we needed to do was to go to the next town where there were several. He told me the name of the town but it meant nothing. So I abandoned that subject and mentioned the towels.

'Ah, yes. I noticed they were missing. I was going to bring them up while you were out.'

'Actually, we need them now.'

He paused. 'I'll ask Michel.'

Five minutes later he appeared with soft, pale blue towels, worth the wait. The inappropriate and sexist thought that a Michelle might have been more towel-orientated briefly crossed my mind, but I rejected the idea.

After searching the map, we found a town that sounded something like the word I'd heard. On the way, Tony spotted a sign saying it was the home of the *véritable tarte tatin*. He immediately forgot about missing towels, the absence of a key and the closed auberge; he couldn't stop grinning with anticipation. We found a lively restaurant, its outside terrace popular with locals who came and went, shaking hands with each other and waving to passing cars as they hooted their horns. When it came to the dessert, the waitress rattled off a short list.

'Is there no tarte tatin?'

'Not tonight.'

Maybe Josephine had the same problem and suffered the same dismay at her wishes being frustrated. We returned to our unlocked room, after just two attempts to get the code on the door to work.

The next morning, we met Daniel in the breakfast room where four places were beautifully laid with fine china and elegant cutlery. The range of homemade jams was impressive and we were treated to almond cake *maison* as well as croissants. We avoided eating the toast as the slices placed on the table were incongruously black; we knew they would be by the smell that preceded them. We were the only ones there, the other two guests in the Red Room in the second tower not having yet appeared. I asked about the history of the house. I think this was the cue Daniel needed, as he settled himself down beside us with his stories. *Bienvenue au Château* had correctly pointed out that English was not spoken so we chatted in French. He had bought the château, presumably with Michel, twenty-five years previously when he was looking for 'something bigger'. It was intact but without electricity or water, a major renovation task. It had indeed belonged to the Beauharnais family, Josephine having lived there in her pre-Napoleonic days with her husband, Alexandre, before the French Revolution took his head. Paying guests were an innovation in the last five years.

'Do you enjoy having visitors?'

'Yes. No problems. Not until today, anyway!' He chuckled at his joke. 'Do you have time to see the original kitchen?'

Of course we had. On the way, we saw the gracious dining room where they had entertained twenty-two for a family baptism. But his favourite was the huge, original kitchen in the cellar. The walls were lined with copper pans and the massive fireplace had the remains of a log fire. In the centre was an old wooden table, polished by the use of many hands. It was the table where Josephine had sat when she signed over the house to her son, Eugène de Beauharnais. She had returned to the house to finalise the papers but had decided not to use the grand rooms upstairs.

209

I stroked the table and felt her fingertips. Who cares about a bit of disorganisation when you get a treat like that?

Mountain Sprouts and Mountain Pockets

It was the first and only time we'd taken a sprout skiing.

Why? Well, there's a story.

We were out skiing with our Welsh friends, Siân and Peter, who also have an apartment in Mottaret. It was a clear, sunny day and as we tightened our boot clips at the top of the Pas du Lac ski lift before descending into Courchevel, I heard laughter. Looking around, the cause was obvious. Three 'ladies' were entertaining the crowd. Attired in flowery dresses and coats, headscarves tied tightly over fluffy hair, they clasped their handbags and adjusted their sunglasses. They preened themselves and stretched their lipsticked mouths.

'Going to the post office to collect our pensions,' one of them said.

'Do you know where the post office is?' another asked.

Then some advice. 'You take care. Make the most of being young!'

One of them handed a card to Siân: 'The skiing Nana's' (with unnecessary apostrophe – author's note).

Their repartee was well-practised in a (pseudo?) Brummie accent. These Nanas have a strong Facebook following, where their odd underwear and odder anatomical parts are on display. They cavort around the ski resorts for no obvious reason other than amusement.

As they prepared to set off on their short skis (the sort that need no ski poles; poles would clearly get in the way of the handbags), one of them handed something that looked like an old-fashioned gobstopper to Siân.

'Have a sweet, dear.'

Ten minutes later, on an almost empty slope, a wild skier decided he needed Siân's bit of piste, falling over and causing her to fall, too. Siân never falls. She hurt her hand, not seriously, but she is a pianist.

We headed for a recuperating drink at a local chalet and Siân put a sprout on the table. We looked at her and stared at it. What kind of fetish was this? It was the 'sweet' from one of the Nanas. Well-formed, a tight little bundle, it was a sweet sprout. It accompanied us for the rest of the day.

When Siân fell getting off a chair-lift, a bruising fall, we began to think something was up. Was this the curse of the sprout? We were worried about a third fall – not that we are superstitious – so stopped for a vin chaud to calm our nerves. The sprout sat on the table again, greenly giving us the evil eye.

That evening, we decided there needed to be a ceremonial discarding of the sprout. One day was enough. We toasted its departure as we had a customary pre-dinner apéritif with our friends. We hoped it took its curse with it. The following day, Peter was hit by a snowboarder. The third event – did he have sprout remains in his pocket? Who knows?

Talking of pockets, a valuable asset is a large one that goes across the back of the ski jacket near the bottom. Its presumed purpose is for carrying spare clothing, a scarf or neckpiece. Tony has one of these. The jacket manufacturers, however, were no doubt unaware of its main use which is as a cheese pocket.

As I've mentioned whenever I could, cheese, especially Beaufort, is one of the delights of the French Alps. By chance, we called in at a small restaurant above Courchevel for a vin chaud and discovered that the couple who run it make their own Beaufort. It's available to as part of a meal, as a tasting platter, or to buy and take away. They usually have cheeses of different ages, and they each make their own so there is family rivalry. And it's a good price. When we first visited, a tasting platter with some bread was offered free with drinks but now they charge. I don't blame them. Their generosity must have made them too popular. Shopping isn't usually a consideration when skiing, but this cheese is delicious. Tony buys a large slab – up to a kilo – which fits beautifully into his back pocket. His balance is rather disturbed and he is conscious of not wanting to arrive home with a pocket of cheese crumbs, but so far, no problem. We are frequent visitors to the *Ferme* and it's hard to resist a tasting. We've corrupted friends and family, too. What's more, they are open in the summer so it's a regular walk. I must stop talking about cheese.

Not Always Alpine Skiing

It wasn't a day for going out on the slopes. Wind, heavy snowfall, mist – more the conditions for reading a book than being outdoors. Then the wind dropped, the snowflakes became smaller and visibility increased. So we decided to do something different and dig out our cross-country skis.

It was a long time since our Norway days when we had frequent cross-country outings and, while never experts, became competent. We'd taken our kit to France but it had remained in our basement cupboard, our *cave*, untouched, for years. No problem, we thought. You never totally forget. However, like a little-used language, such skills wane with time. We set out for a cross-country area by the local lake, the lightweight skis easy to carry and the boots kinder to the feet than the downhill variety. The radio had reported the trails were groomed and there is nothing like a well-prepared track. It holds the ski in a straight line and makes the required stride-and-glide motion easy.

There was some old wax on the bases of the skis from the last time we used them. Waxes are specific to temperature and we had no idea what the conditions were at the last outing. As I've said before, ski-waxing is a black art – in this case, more a dirty grey one – and many hours can be spent getting it right.

'Let's just go with what's on there,' Tony said. 'It'll be okay.' It was the easy option. But the wrong one. We should have cleaned them.

Twenty minutes later, we'd done no skiing. We hadn't even put our skis on. We were still trying to get our boots to attach to the bindings, partially seized up with lack of use. It should be an easy toe-click and in. Should be. I succeeded but then had to remove my skis to help Tony who was struggling. When kneeling beside him and pushing his foot down failed, I tried standing on the toe of his boot. This finally worked and he was shod. Putting my own skis back on was inexplicably more difficult the second time and while I was trying, our Dutch neighbours from the second floor of our chalet walked by. We'd seen them on cross-country skis a couple of days earlier and had smiled to ourselves – not mocked, just smiled – at their wobbles, lack of speed and minimal expertise. After all, hills and the Dutch are not normally associated. It was now their turn as they grinned and walked on by.

Finally, we were ready. We had a small hill to go up and that was no problem. We had plenty of grip – the wax was great. However, once on the flat we realised we had both grown. The snow was building up under our skis to a depth of around 3cm. Platform shoes were once a fashion statement. Platform skis are neither fashionable nor functional. Clearly we had the wrong wax – one for warmer conditions – and could barely plod let alone glide. To make things worse, the perfect tracks we'd been hoping for had filled up with new snow and were little more than minimal indentations. Skis off and scraper out. We removed as much of the grey, sticky stuff as possible and gave the skis a rub with a cork block.

Suffice to say putting the skis back on was no easier the second time. Our Dutch friends, on their way back, waved cheerily to us. They saw us only when we were

215

stationary. Our efforts gained us a marginal increase in speed but not enough so we had to go round the same wretched procedure again. The air was turning blue. At the third time of trying, we made progress. I had some glide – more than Tony, which didn't help matters. Our outing lasted two hours; we skied, after a fashion, for around thirty minutes.

All was not bad, however. There were some positives:

- We didn't fall over
- We used plenty of energy – mostly nervous – and got some exercise
- We gave all our best swear words an outing
- We thought better of the ability of our Dutch friends
- Our skiing could only improve

Although maybe we'd have been more sensible if we'd simply stayed in and read a book.

Our children were amused by our efforts and as a result, bought us some new, waxless skis as a present. Such skis can be used in any conditions and at any temperature, removing all our waxing issues in a flash. When we first skied in Norway, we were sniffy about such skis, being purists about the advantages of getting the waxing just right. Cross-country ski snobs. We'd learned our lesson. Now we were glad of any advantage.

However, removing the excuse that the waxing was wrong meant all our problems were now due to our ability – or lack of it. We were wobbly. Little practice and increasing age? Maybe. Perhaps the old skills will return. I'm trying to persuade Tony that his fear of going down one particular slope is more neurosis after a fall than an inability to stay upright. We both gained a few bruises and Tony a damaged shoulder. There is one bend that defeats us most of the time.

We persevere.

If the nerves aren't up to cross-country struggles, we turn to snow shoes, *raquettes* as they're called. I didn't think I wanted any – they were for folk who don't ski. But they've become popular in the Three Valleys as a means of getting out into the wilds, seeing animal tracks and enjoying nature. So we decided to buy some. They are more streamlined than the old-fashioned ones shaped like tennis racquets. I'd first met those in Norway back in the eighties. We'd been staying with friends in their cabin in the mountains and were essential equipment for going to the outside loo after a heavy snowfall. I imagine I must have looked much like a toddler walking with a full nappy. The modern ones are much easier to walk in with little skill required. Easy to put on, there's just the choice of whether to walk with the heel free or clamped.

We decided one dull day to walk along a newly created raquette route to the Espace Confort, the restaurant where we'd once had a superb meal. We planned a coffee stop there and then a return along a long but easy path. The initial, steep slope was tiring but we made it. The wind got wilder and the visibility decreased so we decided we needed an alternative plan to the long loop we'd planned to do. We knew there was a lift near the restaurant that would take us to the top of the mountain from where we could ride down in a second lift, a quicker, easier and more pleasant way home. As we plodded on, silent, heads down against the gale, a pisteur on a skidoo stopped and asked us where we were going. Sadly, he told us the lifts were closed because of the weather. A couple of skiers shot past us – we were now on a ski slope – and I longed for my skis, too.

We arrived at the restaurant to find the small coffee and snack bar closed. But the main restaurant was open. It was now Plan C. We went in and had a long, pleasant lunch, re-fuelling ourselves for the difficult walk back and re-energised by a glass or two of wine. The conditions were horrible. Snow stung our faces and got in our eyes; progress was slow and the wind held us back. We arrived home exhausted. Maybe we shouldn't reserve snow-shoeing for bad weather days. We need to learn to enjoy it.

The Best Journey Home

There's the direct route – and many others. The best was via Avignon, Nîmes, Carcassonne, Bordeaux, Tours and Honfleur. To call that a route from the Alps to England implies a poor sense of direction but it's worth doing if there's no need to rush. It was our own Grand Tour.

The sharp-eyed will have noticed that it passes through significant wine areas. No accident there. In fact, it was originally a visit to the Bordeaux region and in the planning, grew. Tony, as always, had a spreadsheet. It covered where we were staying each night (usually a *Chambre d'Hôte*, often in the *Logis de France* range) and rough location. Then there was a printout for each with the address and an email confirming the booking. He is organised so I don't have to be.

It went wrong on the way to Avignon. The printout for the *Logis* for that evening was missing. Tony insisted he had taken it out of the file ready for use and I vaguely recalled he'd been waving a piece of paper around. We had a rummage – ruck-sack pockets, trouser pockets, pockets in the doors of the car – without success.

'No problem,' Tony insisted. 'The name's on the spreadsheet. We just need to google it to find the address.'

So I did just that and we found the place.

Congratulating ourselves, we went to reception. They had no record of our booking. And they were full. As the queue grew behind us, Madame did a lot of clicking on her computer, a lot of searching in a paper file and a lot of puffing.

'Do you have a confirmation of your booking?'

Of course, we did, if only we knew where the damn thing was. Then Tony had an inspiration and found the secretive piece of paper in the side pocket of a previously unsearched hold-all.

'Ah!' she exclaimed, breaking into a smile of relief. 'This is not us!'

We were at the wrong Logis.

Tony then remembered he'd been unable to book his first choice so had found somewhere else. But he hadn't updated the spreadsheet. We need to take senior moments into account in our travelling. We set off to the correct Logis, which turned out to be far better than the first. It was hot, over 30 degrees, and the swimming pool tempted us in.

We loved Avignon – apart from the parking. It should be an Olympic sport, it's so difficult. Roads are made for small cars, 2CVs. So are the underground car parks. We don't have a 2CV. We did what all tourists do and went *sur le pont* – the part-pont, as only a small amount of it remains. I expected the famous song to be playing and at least someone to be dancing. Wrong. So on the way back, we sang a few lines of it, quietly to ourselves. If you've ever heard us sing, you'll know why. We passed on the dancing; we didn't want to be too ostentatious. However, the town recognises the importance of that simple ditty. It has brought more visitors to Avignon than any advertising campaign could ever have done.

Evening Avignon was beautiful. The main square by the Palais des Papes was flooded with gentle sunlight and a choir entertained the crowds with a mixture of Gospel and

Rock. We looked down on the rooftops, all pale terracotta or brownish-cream. The houses were cream, too, with dark red shutters. We liked the pleasing uniformity and were glad to be there. The following day we visited the Palais; the nine popes who lived there knew how to look after themselves.

I have no idea how many Bordeaux vineyards there are. A quick search on Google told me it wasn't worth trying to find out. So when we decided on a three-night stop in the region, giving us two days for wine tasting, we didn't know where to begin. Having booked a pleasant *Chambre d'Hôte* not far from St Emilion, we asked the advice of the owner, Michel, and he came up trumps. We'd explained that we wanted to buy some wine – some good wine – but were not expecting to spend our life's savings on it (you can!) He understood. He proposed a small selection, indicated the price range of the wines and what tastings they could provide. We selected two in the St Emilion area (on the right bank of the Dordogne) and two in Medoc (on the left bank). They say the best vines are grown within sight of the river; the most expensive are.

Our first St Emilion vineyard was Château Mangot. They are all Châteaux even if there is no building worthy of the name. Mangot is smallish and smart, totally modernised, state-of-the-art stainless steel vats, new oak barrels. We had a personal guide who spoke exceedingly fast French. When it came to the technicalities of wine production, he saw our puzzled faces and changed to much slower and somewhat halting English which suited us fine. Lovely wine. Tony regretted he was driving and sighed as he savoured a mouthful or two and tipped the rest away. We bought a few bottles, of course.

The town of St Emilion is pretty, hilly and full of people. It also has an underground world of interesting monuments. We enjoyed lunch in the town and bought some good value wine in one of the many shops offering tastings before setting off for the Château de Pressac for the afternoon *dégustation*. This was a far bigger place, looking like an old château, with timed tours and more commercialisation. State-of-the-art, again. We bought our wine-loving son-in-law his birthday present. As we drove back to our B & B, in a temperature of 36°C, we hoped we weren't cooking it.

We learned that the wine has to be more than 50% Merlot to be classified as *St Emilion*. Conversely, *Médoc* wines have to contain more than 50% Cabernet Sauvignon. We learned an awful lot more, too, but it passes in and out again, interesting and pleasurable at the time but transient, much like the wine. In St Emilion, the Grand Cru classifications are assessed every ten years or so, based on quality. However, the classification of Médoc wines dates from 1855, established by Napoleon III. Fine for those at the top, but the system hasn't changed since then and new vineyards, however good their wines, cannot be called Grand Cru or Grand Cru Classé. We felt that there was a touch of the Emperor's New Clothes in the naming and pricing of the wines here – it has to be good because of its ancient appellation. A more recent Médoc classification, the Cru Bourgeois, must be applied for and earned annually. How sensible!

Our Médoc visits next, Château de Paloumey and Château Mayne Lalande; a few more purchases. Bordeaux has to compete with the new world wines; they can't just rely on reputation. Nevertheless, we felt we had to go and at least look at the vineyards of one of the Great Names. It was closed for August (and would never be open for folk like us) but I did manage to taste a very young wine. Most people would call it a grape. Yes, I stole a ripe grape! In order to protect the guilty, I won't say which vineyard it was. But think somewhere in the Margaux area …

We ate in Bordeaux that evening, overlooking the river. Michel and Annie at the B & B made the booking for us. We must revisit this beautiful city when we have more time. We left the following day. But not before, Michel, who has a well-stocked cellar of his own, sold us a few bottles ...

Then our last stop – Honfleur. Artists used to come here for the inspiration it gave them and the particular light found in this port on the north coast of France where the Seine meets the sea. We came to see the steep, cobbled streets and the squashed, crooked houses along the quayside, sometimes eight times as high as they are wide. The Quartier St Leonard was previously the artists' area and their legacy remains. You cannot walk far without finding ateliers and shops selling paintings and sculptures. There is a school of Graphic Art. It is also the place to stay and our *Chambre d'Hôte* was an eclectic place full of the quirky and unusual, a metal dragonfly on our wall, embroidered lace slips on our pillows. Curious details in hidden corners. Plus a delicious breakfast.

Rain pelted us with giant spots on our trip around town – we ran from Monet to Baudelaire. Then on to a French king, a scientist, a novelist as the squall passed through the *Parc des Personalités*. Puffs of grey and white cloud, blown up from nowhere, blocked the sunshine. It had been a bright day but now we needed shelter. Then minutes later, the sun was out again.

Food was a theme and we were spoiled by the variety of seafood. Unfortunately, my husband won't eat creatures that live in shells so the magnificent platters were banned in favour of fresh fish. We ate at the delightfully named Absynthe, perhaps a reflection of the drinking habits of the bohemians who visited Honfleur in the past. I looked but couldn't find the spirit on the drinks list.

We could, however, find plenty of Calvados and

223

Normandy cider. We learned that an eight-year-old Calvados is still 'young' – rough fire-water to burn the throat. If you can afford to buy a twenty-five-year-old bottle, that's a taste worth savouring. We also learned something about cider, that *sec* is drier than *brut* and that it will keep about a year (although not in our hands).

Near the elegant Hôtel de Ville was a permanently sited carousel. I usually dislike these tacky entertainments but this one from 1900 was two-tiered and immaculate. There was a constant stream of riders keen to mount the horses rising and falling to appropriately muted fairground music. This was typical of Honfleur. It seems to have avoided the tat that seaside towns everywhere adore. Even the second-hand market on Sunday morning had a classy air about it. Sure there are tourists and the English make up many but it is also a resort for the French. It is a comfortable place where huge pleasure comes from sitting in a street café, drinking coffee or something stronger and watching the activities of passers-by.

We were drawn to the Musée Eugène Boudin to see the impressionist paintings. It wasn't just good weather that attracted artists to Honfleur. The town was captured by them in all its moods and colours. Brilliant sunshine to grey, stormy skies – much as we had seen and enjoyed it.

We understood the inspiration. We were comfortable there – and comfortable in France.

The Inevitable

I've had my share of ski accidents – more than anyone else in the family. I've probably had everyone else's share, too. Am I a risk-prone skier? A bad skier who always finds themselves in someone's way? Or just unlucky?

My right knee was dodgy, I knew that. The result of assorted ligament injuries over many years, not to mention a broken bone. But, generally, it didn't affect my skiing. Occasionally, well away from the slopes, my knee would lock and become painful to move. I would have to straighten it slowly until an audible click told me it was functioning again. It was a noise that made Tony shudder. Can't say I liked it either but it was a necessary manoeuvre. It happened at strange times: getting out of the car, wriggling around on the floor with a grandchild, bending awkwardly.

One sunny day, we were skiing down an easy but interesting blue slope towards Mottaret when my knee locked. I didn't fall but it hurt so I slid to a halt. Tony was ahead and stopped to see where I was. He knew exactly my problem as I tried to straighten my leg. The reassuring click would not happen. I removed my skis and tried again. No joy. Tony climbed back up towards me – fortunately, it wasn't steep – and I explained, not that he needed any explanation.

'Could I ski down on one ski? I can still walk.'

'No way. It's a fair distance and unless you have speed, there are a couple of humps you'd never get over. I think I'd better go and get the blood wagon.'

My third blood wagon. One in Norway and two in France. That's three too many. Tony skied on down and I stood beside the slope, persevering unsuccessfully in my attempts to straighten my leg. The kindness of passing skiers was touching. Many stopped and asked if I needed help. The blood wagon and its driver arrived and I was able to climb onto the sledge with a little assistance. It was the usual uncomfortable ride. Every so often a passing skier would peer in to see if I was alive.

By the time we reached the Medical Centre in Mottaret, I'd stiffened up. I was moved onto the bed where the doctor asked me to bend my swelling knee in ways I didn't want to. I rewarded him with a number of shouts. Seems I'd ruptured a cartilage. A knee brace, rest, painkillers and daily injections of an anti-coagulant (which I learned to do myself) became the prospect for the rest of my winter.

Back in the UK, an MRI scan confirmed the French doctor's diagnosis. I expected him to be right; he'd seen it all before. The surgeon said he could operate but it was my choice; it wasn't life-threatening. I caught sight of my reflection in a shop window – a bent back and walking with a limp. I looked like one of the traffic signs sometimes seen by old people's homes warning you there may be frail, doddery folk about. The choice was simple.

'Will you repair the cartilage?'

I'd done my internet search and knew this was a possibility.

'No. I'll remove it. You can manage without it. If you were twenty-one and played professional football, I'd do the repair.'

That put me my place.

'Will I be able to ski afterwards?'

'If you want to ski, you'll be able to.'

He was right, of course. The following season, with Tony following ('to pick up the pieces'), I got back into my normal rhythm. In January, my nervousness gradually disappeared. By March, I was getting my speed back and feeling confident.

Then I had a stupid fall getting off a chair lift and twisted the left knee, the good one. We were in Val Thorens, nearly as far away as we could be from our apartment. But I made it back. It wasn't the end of the story as much physiotherapy followed. But I'm stubborn (ask Tony about it) and I wasn't about to stop skiing. What is it that comes before a fall, according to the old saying?

A couple of months later, coming down an empty, wide slope, I was suddenly catapulted into the air, lost both skis and landed on my left knee. A young man, skiing well but too fast, had been unable to avoid me. Unapologetic, he said I skied into his path. I probably did but it was his responsibility to avoid me as I was below him – a basic mountain rule. He had plenty of available slope. Tony reckoned he was showing off to his girlfriend and possibly under the influence of something or other. Yet again, I got up and skied on but knees can only take so much. It hasn't stopped me but it's slowed me down.

The inevitable. If accidents don't slow you down, then age surely will. We are fair-weather skiers now, enjoying the blue skies and sunshine; being able to see where we are going. We have no need to ski in a blizzard; there are other things to do. And our days have got shorter. Rarely are we at the lifts before they open and we are never at the top of the mountain when they close. A long morning, with a pleasant vin chaud stop, and then back to the apartment for a late lunch suits us fine. I never thought I'd admit to this. But, actually, I'm not ashamed of it. Some of our friends have, sadly, given up skiing; we are fortunate enough to be able to carry on.

There are other changes, too, since we embarked on our ski-bumming career, some outside our control. Lifts have been upgraded or replaced. There are fewer slow, drag lifts – reminiscent of Norway – and chair lifts may now reward you with a warmed seat. You can get to the highest point in the area more quickly now. Picnic tables have proliferated and if you prefer to eat in, there are new, modern, mountain restaurants with tasty food and good service. We lose each other less often as we now carry mobile phones; there are hot-spots everywhere. We've got new favourite restaurants – Le Martagon in Nantgerel, between Méribel and Moûtiers where they serve the best frogs' legs you'll find. And as a treat, Le Farçon in La Tania for a Michelin-starred lunch. Unusual food, relaxing ambiance and, while not cheap, well worth the money.

On the downside, the removal of the old, uncomfortable, two-man chair out of Courchevel is probably not grieved by many but it was a convenient way home and we miss it. The end of the wonderful crêperie in Courchevel where we doused our pancakes in a sea of Grand Marnier, the closure of the welcoming restaurant, Crêtes, on the ridge above Méribel (although a swish replacement now sits there), the incorporation of Au Temps Perdu, a favourite underground restaurant in Mottaret, into a local hotel are something we simply have to put up with. Many bars have opened, provided interesting evenings out, and closed in that time; the resorts evolve. I now respect the old gentleman's views and always walk in proper boots. On arrival at the Refuge du Saut, I use the proper plumbed-in toilet. We have a small washing machine in the bathroom – bye-bye, laverie! We've made local friends, are known in many of the shops.

It feels like home; it is home.

Closure – but we'll be back

(We have to – our age means the ski passes will be free!)

It was the middle of March, 2020. Perfect corduroy stripes on the mountain. No ski tracks, either good or bad. A couple of teenagers walking up the slope carrying sledges, jumping on them and sliding down. A treat – sledges aren't normally allowed on the pistes. Smaller kids with plastic skid-pans playing on the sledging slope. The sky was deep blue with the tiniest wisp of cloud near the horizon. No wind. It would be glorious to sit outside a mountain restaurant, drink in hand, jacket off, sun cream on.

It was hard work plodding across the snow, soft, almost slushy, cut up by the passage of many feet. Here and there a piste machine had flattened it but the smooth surface didn't last long. We headed for the lake, Lac de Tueda, for a walk, planning to follow the cross-country trail that rises above it, circles it and then drops back down. I'd never seen so many people here. Every bench had its occupants. A finely made snow-hole, almost an igloo, attracted children on their hands and knees. The supermarket must have done a good trade in beer judging by the number of bottles in hands. Picnic time – cheese and salami spread out on pieces of paper, baguettes roughly torn into pieces. A party atmosphere. Almost a party atmosphere.

A couple of cross-country skiers went past. The perfect tracks cut daily had all but gone in spite of notices telling pedestrians not to walk along them. Hard work without them – or plenty of skill. A couple of skiers appeared wearing normal alpine skis. Where had they come from? No lifts were working so they must have plodded up. Not worth it, I thought, but it must have been for them.

Enterprising, closed restaurants were selling takeaway meals. A service, a way for them to make some money and not waste their stock. Some even had food going free – just help yourself. I'd taken a piece of salami and eaten it. Then thought how silly I was taking the risk. This wasn't a familiar situation.

Ski shops were open for the return of hire equipment but not for sales. Except for the odd cheat – a rail of discounted goods outside one shop. Who would find out? It was there just for a few hours. I hope they sold something even though they broke the rules. There would be no end-of-season sales this year.

The car parks, full to capacity a day ago, were emptying. We overheard conversations about difficulties in getting transport out of the valley and the problems with airlines. We'd changed our ferry booking and were heading for Calais by car in two days' time. I'd concocted some paperwork, based on what I thought might be needed. Written in English and French and signed by us both, it would at least show we'd tried. The new rules meant you needed documentation to justify any outing, even walking a dog. Surely France would be glad to see us go and not make our journey difficult. What would greet us in England? We didn't know but felt we should get back while we could. Goodbye, Méribel Mottaret. See you next in better times. We'll be back – but when?

The chaos of the arrival of the corona virus.

For info - Where did we stay?

These are some of the interesting places we stayed on our trips through France.

Château de Gilly, Vougeot, Burgundy
A grand castle decorated in traditional French style. Superb restaurant in the vaulted cellar.

Gentilhommière, Nuits St Georges
A sixteenth century Hunting Lodge. The bedrooms, not in the old, main building, are modern and stylish.

Château de Pizay, Beaujolais
A 4* hotel and spa, situated in its own vineyard. Gourmet restaurant.

Château d'Etoges, near Epernay, Champagne
Family-owned, seventeenth century castle, listed as a historic monument. Gourmet restaurant, L'Orangerie. (Note – since our visit, they have opened a brasserie-style restaurant, L'Atelier.)

Château de la Verrerie, Oizon, Loire et Cher

Beautiful 'fairy castle', classified as an historic monument. Château and park open to the public/guided tours. Good restaurant, Maison d'Hélène.

Château de la Ferté Beauharnais, Sologne

Privately owned small château, quirky, interesting. Partly fifteenth, partly eighteenth century, it was owned by the Beauharnais family (Josephine). Has four rooms only, bed and breakfast, no restaurant.

Logis de France

A huge number of properties throughout France. Usually comfortable and good value for money. Most have restaurants.

About the Author

Linda has always enjoyed writing although for many years, work as an industrial pharmacist got in the way. Since she retired, she has been able to indulge this passion and writes fiction, non-fiction and occasional poetry.

She has published two novels, 'A Taste of his Own Medicine' and 'A Prescription for Madness', both using her background in pharmacy. This is her first non-fiction book.

Skiing is a passion equal to writing and this is shared by the whole family – her husband, her three children, their husbands/wives and the seven grandchildren.

Linda lives in Winnersh, Berkshire with her husband, Tony.

Printed in Great Britain
by Amazon